Dear Dave,   Jan. 24, '06

Thank you for spending time with us and sharing your strategic insights during the interview.

Hope to see you in near future.

All the Best!

Hiro

DESIGNED TO WIN

DESIGNED TO WIN

Strategies for Building a Thriving Global Business

Hiroaki Yoshihara
Mary Pat McCarthy

McGraw-Hill

New York   Chicago   San Francisco   Lisbon
London   Madrid   Mexico City   Milan
New Delhi   San Juan   Seoul
Singapore   Sydney   Toronto

Contents

Acknowledgments

To build a thriving and enduring global business, demands extraordinary and visionary leadership. It is a quality that distinguished each of the global executives we interviewed for this book. For their insights and time, we are deeply indebted to: Stefan Krause, CFO of BMW Group; Jim Owens and Dave Burritt, respective CEO and CFO of Caterpillar Inc.; Arvind Sodhani, President of Intel Capital; Kunio Nakamura, President of Matsushita Electric Industrial and Katsuaki Watanabe, President of Toyota Motor Corporation.

We are also sincerely grateful to our fellow partners and colleagues for their strong support, enthusiasm and contributions: Weronika Anasz, Stanley Anders, Dan Doherty, Michael Fath, Timothy Flynn, Michael Hagenhoff, Johann Höfer, Megumu Komikado, Dale LeMasters, Masahiro Mekada, Sangeeta Schneider-Wadhwani, Scott Showalter, Catherine Taranto, Julian Thomas and Mark Walton.

Special thanks to the unwavering commitment of Marie Glenn, the enthusiasm and support of McGraw-Hill, Kim van der Meij for keeping the project on track and Maureen Migliazzo for her sound judgment and project direction.

Hiroaki Yoshihara
Mary Pat McCarthy
November 2005

Introduction

The only constant is change, so goes the adage. That being so, a corporate leader must nimbly navigate its currents. Management has always required this degree of skill and dexterity. What is different and inherently more challenging about today's business environment is that not only is the operating environment changing, but so too the modes of operating within it. It is a difficult but exciting time for global executives.

Globalization is choreographing much of the sea change. There are more market participants, more products, more competitors, more opportunities for success and an equal number for failure. The rise of China and India is testing the traditional hegemony of the west while emerging competitors are challenging conventional wisdom about expanding and marketing in the developing world. Which strategy will serve one's market entry and operations purposes best? Business leaders face complex choices in determining the answer, with foreign direct investment, joint ventures, outsourcing, mergers, acquisitions and other forms of partnership among the many available options.

The increased connectivity and interdependency of the global marketplace places additional responsibilities in the hands of business men and women. They must be commercial diplomats as well as corporate leaders. They must deliver value to their shareholders and demonstrate strong social commitment to their communities. They must provide globally consistent quality while satisfying a multiplicity of customer needs. They must promote a uniform global brand while presenting a local market face. They must drive financial and operating efficiencies across their enterprise while at the same time adapting to new opportunities and changes in the market.

In light of these dizzying responsibilities, the primary global leadership challenge may well be to maintain discipline and focus in the midst of chaos. Such unflappability is a demonstrated prerequisite for those who serve at the senior ranks of any multinational company. As they and managers everywhere confront the changing face of competition, this book offers guidance on what it takes to build a strong and enduring global business, a business that is *Designed to Win*.

We hope you enjoy.

Sincerely,

Hiroaki Yoshihara

Mary Pat McCarthy

November 2005

CHAPTER 1

Winning in the Global Arena

"The driving force behind globalization is free market capitalization—the more you let free market forces rule and the more you open your economy to free trade and competition, the more efficient and flourishing your economy will be. Globalization means the spread of free market capitalization to virtually every country in the world."

—Thomas L. Friedman,
author of *The Lexus and the Olive Tree*

Technology, trade and economic liberalization, each formidable in their own right, have combined to exact an extraordinary pull on the average multinational corporation. Free market policies, formerly the purview of developed nations, are lapping onto the shores of other nations, increasingly those found in the developing world. Trade regulation is loosening the still firm north-south divide. Protectionism, ever present, is falling into wider disfavor.

Together, the forces of globalization are propelling a new age of radical competition. The way in which companies innovate, source materials, and distribute and market goods and services is altering the manner in which skilled competitors, both entrenched and new, are arriving at cheaper, faster and better products and services.

What does it take to win in our new global arena? What characteristics will define the likeliest survivors and what will be the shape of the radically evolving environment in which they operate? These are the questions this book seeks to address, equipped with our own experiences in serving multinational corporations and, importantly, supplemented with commentary from the business leaders charged with steering them forward.

As a backdrop to these questions, this chapter looks at the impact of globalization on the world's economy and its emergence as a primary force in shaping modern competition.

EARLY ROOTS OF GLOBALIZATION

The earliest "globalists" and traders were soldiers, sailors, prophets and enterprising wanderers. In some cases, their motivation tied to human desires for stability and comfort, and in others, the pursuit of knowledge and prosperity. Collectively, these needs have spurred interest in travel, adventure and conquest since the dawn of time.

Evidence of active trading in spices, gold, textiles and

other precious commodities has been found along the Arabian Peninsula as early as 3000 BC. In the Canadian province of Manitoba, copper from Lake Superior and shells from the Gulf of Mexico were found dating back to 500 BC. In the second century, well-worn routes along the east coast of Africa were regularly plied by traders exchanging goods. In time, expanding empires from the Assyrians to the Romans allowed the influx of culture to flow across borders.

The industrial age ushered in a new desire for raw materials sourced from far flung global outposts. In Europe, rubber from South America and Asia was turned into waterproof clothing, equipment and consumer products. Later, this same rubber was "vulcanized" by the American Charles Goodyear, and molded into tires, changing forever the course of modern transportation. Other valuable goods, such as copper ore, lumber and oil, fueled a groundswell of industry, bolstered trade and strengthened international ties.

EMERGING POWERS

Over time, reliance on key supplies and customers led to a growing interdependence between nations and a shift in power structures. In the rapidly developing Western world, wealth grew, cities expanded and business prospered. The rise of the middle class and improved forms of transportation, from shipping to the automobile, fostered strides in economic growth and increased consumption of globally produced goods.

Globalization

The term globalization took formal root in the English language in the early 1960s, but was popularized by Theodore Leavitt, a Harvard Business School professor who used it as the basis of his 1983 article entitled, "The Globalization of Markets." The modern definition of globalization refers to increased economic integration and interdependence, as well as a rising volume of capital and trade movement brought on by lower transportation, communications and labor costs. The term also refers to the world's social organization and the growth of an emerging global consciousness.

The West's burgeoning military-industrial infrastructure and financial wealth led to a growing influence in global affairs. While the Cold War amplified the divergence between open-market and closed-market ideals, Western principles of democracy, representative government, free speech and free trade continued to spread. The collapse of the Berlin Wall and communism in Eastern Europe during the 1990s offered both symbolic and tangible evidence of the pull of capitalism and Western political thought, particularly among a repressed people. The wave of democracy building since then has allowed individuals around the world to have a greater say in national and global policy making. Today, 140 of the world's nearly 200 countries hold democratic, multi-party elections.

TECHNOLOGICAL SEA CHANGE

With trade, democracy and free market ideals on the march around the world, it needed only the flashpoint of ubiquitous computing and communications to cause the modern concept of globalization to explode onto the world scene. When Samuel Morse heralded the arrival of the telegraph with his famous question, "What hath God wrought?" he could have had no idea of the magnitude of future telecommunications on global society.

The availability of these technologies has literally altered the course of history. Witness the breaking of ENIGMA during World War II. The cracking of the sophisticated German machine cipher was one of the most profound events in the entire history of secret writing. The ability to decipher Axis code during the early years of World War II saved tens of thousands of Allied lives and played a major role in the winning the war.

The lack of technology also had severe consequences even further back. In the futile battle of New Orleans during the War of 1812, hundreds of lives were lost in a fight that could have been averted had news of the Treaty of Ghent, signaling the War's end, arrived more quickly. Instead, the news traveled by ship in a slow journey that took two weeks too long.

As a catalyst for commerce, democratization, cultural transformation and knowledge sharing, modern day communications have no rival. Since the early 1990s, use of the Internet worldwide has surged to over 800 million people. Now the availability of real-time, 24/7 information enables unprecedented productivity and collaboration, allowing previously unheralded partnerships of people to form globally. Technology has emerged as a primary force in the speed and scale of modern globalization. Indeed, as Princeton historian

Harold James observed, technology has rendered inefficient those markets with a purely national focus and has naturally encouraged the spread of commerce to other nations and markets.

THE CONTROVERSY OVER MODERN-DAY GLOBALIZATION

In recent times, globalization has become a lightning rod, noted more for polarizing the world's citizenry than for uniting them. In the eyes of its detractors, globalization is viewed as the means by which powerful multinational companies, most Western, the majority American, enrich themselves at the expense of the poorer countries with whom they seek to open trade. Some of these corporations have also come under fire by critics who point to what they view as shoddy overseas labor practices and negligence with respect to social and environmental obligations.

Intergovernmental bodies like the World Trade Organization (WTO), the International Monetary Fund (IMF) and the World Bank are also in the eye of the storm, even as their member nations grow. One of the more recent examples of a groundswell of opposition to globalization was the unexpectedly violent and disruptive protests at the 1999 Seattle World Trade Organization Ministerial Conference. Critics accuse these organizations of playing into the hands of wealthy nations and failing to adequately deliver the promised benefits of globalization to the developing world.

In this uneven and sometimes rocky fashion, globalization has emerged to take its modern form. Bit by bit, the lines of polarization between supporters and opponents of globalization are softening. Emotional responses are becoming less strident and, to a degree, more irrelevant. As it sheds its thornier edges, globalization is being seen more clearly for what it is—part of a natural, if turbulent, process that will not be turned back.

This being so, the question then becomes not whether globalization is good or bad, but how can it be improved? As a disturbing force, globalization creates a sometimes uncomfortable transparency for both rich and poor, contrasting the dramatic wealth of the developed world with the suffering and poverty of emerging nations. The gap reveals a wide ranging set of issues to be addressed by the global community, from business and economic to social issues.

GLOBALIZATION AND GLOBAL COMPETITIVENESS

Imagine that you are the CEO of a powerful multi-national corporation. In that position, you would rightfully wish to deliver a satisfactory return to your shareholders. Because your company is already very large, double-digit growth is hard to sustain, albeit still an attractive goal. You have operations, joint ventures, contractors, distributors and outsourcers in many foreign locations. Though it is challenging to keep everything and everyone humming the same tune, you rely on the efficiencies and scale of your global enterprise to give you an advantage over traditional rivals and emerging upstarts.

In the case of your Brazilian market, you are heavily dependent on your distributor network. As a dollar-based company, you sell your product in American Dollars and then the distributors sell to the end customer in Brazilian Reals. The arrangement works great until the bottom falls out of the Real. Your distributors, who like most, operate on razor thin margins, either go bankrupt or sit tight on remaining inventory, refusing to buy anything further from you until prices rise. As a consequence, your market share decreases and so does the return you are expecting from your Brazilian portfolio.

Another division has plans to open a heavy manufacturing plant in Southeast Asia. The business, which should benefit the local economy through the hiring of hundreds of workers, will also offer tremendous cost savings to its parent. It is a win-win situation—until a couple of nongovernmental organizations (NGOs) protest the developments fearing the damage they feel the plant will inflict on the environment. Pictures of toxic runoff and negative air quality studies released by the media further sully the company's reputation. The project gets delayed while the company negotiates with the local government, community spokespeople and NGOs to address the matter.

No matter, you are too busy pursuing a lucrative expansion into Russia. You field a highly trained team from your

Austrian and German satellites. Their scouting missions indicate you should have no trouble hiring educated and qualified local staff in Moscow that know the language, bureaucracy, political system and customs. Data show that the burgeoning Russian market is ripe for your information technology products. Unfortunately, six months into your operation, it has become apparent that your local suppliers are controlled by a rogue element with interests in a competing IT business. They withhold two pre-paid orders and deliver an ultimatum to you: pay double or close down. You approach the authorities, but the legal and judicial systems are unable to enforce your contract.

This is a dicey situation. Your third-quarter earnings report is due and the financial markets have been unforgiving. The stock will take a beating if you fall two cents short of expectations, as you anticipate, given your global issues. As you reflect on this, you scan the latest edition of a popular business weekly. The cover shows an angry mob of anti-global protestors holding signs reading, "Down with the Fortune 500," "The World Bank—Puppet of the Rich," and similar slogans. You sigh, thinking, if only you had the power they imagined you had, you wouldn't be in the jam you were in.

These scenarios illustrate a certain undeniable new reality. To win in today's global arena involves far more than making sure the functional processes necessary to produce the traditional widget are in place. To a large extent, today's CEO must not only be a business leader, but a business statesperson.

ACCEPTING A BROADER
LEADERSHIP ROLE

Although business leaders have traditionally been loath to delve into policy matters (after all, isn't that the job of elected officials, chambers of commerce and other bodies?), seasoned professionals are recognizing that it is in their company's best interests to broaden their leadership role. The reason is simple. Sound trade policy improves the competitive environment and furthers corporate growth prospects. As former president of the Philippines, Fidel Ramos, once said, "The peace and prosperity of the rich depend on the well-being of the poor."

Business leaders already have a sizable brief simply dealing with their company's day-to-day economic viability. Added to that, management must respond to the keen need to attract superior talent while adapting to advances in technology and business organization that continue to shrink the impact of geographic and time zone differences, allowing the travel and exchange of goods, people and ideas at low cost and high speed. Small wonder then, that much CEO attention is spent on inward-facing business concerns.

Still, this hefty, if narrow, management view will likely not suffice going forward. In his book, *The Mind of the CEO*, Jeffrey Garten, former investment banker, White House trade official, and former dean of the Yale School of Management, notes several reasons why CEOs should consider a broader leadership role.

Their wider involvement will:

❑ Supplement the insufficient resources of governments and international bodies that lack the training or talent to fill the "regulatory vacuum" at the international level.

❑ Maximize prospects for finding and retaining customers and employees.

❑ Address concerns that unless "CEOs play a leading role in fashioning sensible pro-market arrangements, there will either be increasing chaos in world markets or ill-conceived government regulations, or some combination of both."

❑ Deal with the likelihood that multinationals "risk becoming targets of resentment for both groups and citizens who see globalization as a negative trend."[1]

To create an environment where global competitiveness can further the cause of business will likely require intergovernmental organizations and multinational companies to re-examine economic policies, review the quality of developing domestic institutions, and consider international loan and aid structures that advance the participation of a greater share of the world's people.

To further their own competitive prospects, business leaders, particularly those at large corporations, should consider expanding their duties to include the role of statesman. This includes not only appropriate "good citizen" behaviors, but also a stepped up involvement in encouraging pragmatic reforms that address kinks in current systems of world trade.

UPDATING THE CENTRAL TENETS OF GLOBALIZATION

The main pillars of global competitiveness rely on: trade liberalization, which refers to the increased circulation of goods and services; financial liberalization, which refers to the increased circulation of capital; and, economic liberalization or foreign direct investment, in which companies based in one country make investments to establish and run business operations in another country or countries.

The belief was that those developing nations that adopted a formula of open markets, free trade and liberalization would experience greater economic growth and rising income levels. The experience of the last few decades, however, shows that this formula is not the complete panacea once thought.

TRADE LIBERALIZATION IS NOT A UNIFORM SOLUTION

One startling fact is that the countries that have most successfully integrated into the global economy are not necessarily the ones who have embraced these central principles. China and India have been huge success stories, but their success might have come in spite of globalization, not because of it.

Whereas world bodies such as the IMF and the World Bank have often demanded trade reforms to spur economic growth, China and India's histories suggest the causality may be more tenuous. Both China and India maintain extremely high trade restrictions. Recent moves to reform trade laws have come only after years of strong economic growth. In some respects, China's central market policies perversely paved the way for high growth.

For instance, China's period of high growth started in the late 1970s with the introduction of sweeping economic reforms that aligned and fostered agricultural and industrial development and productivity. The government turned to trade liberalization only when China's economic engine was in full throttle.

Nonetheless, since both India and China do conduct massive amounts of international trade, each is considered a successful example of globalization by World Bank standards. This is in contrast to the experience of many early developing countries, including Vietnam, Taiwan, South Korea and other Asian nations. Their histories suggest that trade liberalization is not frequently an important catalyst for growth and trade, when the country is in the early stages of economic expansion.[2] As Dani Rodrik, Harvard University Professor of International Political Economy, noted, "Rapid integration into global markets is a consequence, not of trade liberalization or adherence to WTO strictures per se, but of successful growth strategies with often highly idiosyncratic characteristics."[3]

In light of the financial crises that rocked Asia and South America at the end of the 20th century, business leaders and governmental organizations alike should consider a more flexible menu of trade reform, one that allows some nations greater permission to build supportive domestic institutions, as well as legal and financial policies that reduce the risks of financial crisis, before mandating more severe austerity programs.

GLOBALIZATION MAY BE THE GREAT EQUALIZER, BUT ONLY FOR THOSE WITH A SEAT AT THE TABLE

United Nations Secretary General Kofi Annan once said, "The poor are not poor because of globalization but because of too little globalization, because they are not part of it, because they are excluded."

Part of the modern idea of globalization is the access it is supposed to provide less developed nations to the international market. The reality has been different. The majority of international trade occurs between developed nations, not between developed and developing ones. According to the United Nations Conference on Trade and Development (UNCTAD), despite the fact that exports from developing nations have grown faster than the world average over the past 20 years, their share of world trade value has increased at a slower rate. That is because while the developed world witnessed a decline in their share of manufacturing exports over the same period, their share of world manufacturing value-added increased. The UNCTAD Trade and Development Report 2002 acknowledges this disparity, stating, "While the share of developing countries in world manufacturing exports, including those of rapidly growing high-tech products, has been expanding rapidly, the income earned from such activities does not appear to share in this dynamism."[4]

Part of the problem stems from the difficulty in attracting the same levels of Foreign Direct Investment. Many developing countries vie with each other as bases for foreign capital. While the stock markets have embraced emerging markets, capital market investments tend to be volatile and narrowly directed to a certain class of emerging market country. Though welcome and important, the unpredictability of these investments makes planning difficult.

Perhaps perversely, the most needed trade swap is that concerning the balance of protectionist provisions. Developing nations are generally far more dependent on commodity exports than richer nations. Their exports often face high tariff protections from established economies, provisions that perpetuate a less than equal playing field.

For example, tariffs imposed on finished textile products, as opposed to raw materials such as cotton which command low value, make them less competitive in major markets like the United States, where trade provisions favor domestic goods. Similarly, while agricultural subsidies have fallen into disfavor, they have not gone away. In contrast to the farm aid provided by European and American governments, many poorer countries cannot afford to subsidize their agriculture sectors in a way that enables them to compete with subsidized exports. Rich countries, in particular the U.S. and the European Union, still spend six to seven times their foreign aid allocations on their own domestic agriculture industries.[5]

To rectify these imbalances, market leaders need to collaborate on ways to offer increased trade protections for the developing world and further reduce those favoring rich nations. New, finished-product industries, like textiles, offer a promising avenue for growth, yet they require lead-time and assistance to ramp up and sustain. Protections that shield valuable but emerging domestic industries from the abrasive forces of global competition would give developing countries the chance to compete without instantly being buffeted to the ground.

Protection waivers in the case of intellectual property rights also need to be considered. In AIDS ravaged sub-Saharan Africa, governments are prohibited from developing cheaper retro-viral medications because of existing copyright law. Temporary exemptions from certain of these intellectual property rules would give poorer nations greater flexibility in combating AIDS and other life-threatening illnesses that afflict their populations.

The private sector is getting more engaged. For example, the Bill & Melinda Gates Foundation is funding research and clinical trials for the AIDS vaccine. If a treatment is identified, the Foundation will secure the vaccine at a modest price and make it available to the developing world. Similar initiatives are underway in other sectors and will be increasingly important to redress global financial and social imbalances.

PROSPERITY IMPROVES PROSPECTS FOR PEACE AND STABILITY

While growth rates in many developing countries have surged, the incomes of many of the world's people have not grown as much as the World Bank and similar organizations had expected. In contrast, the strictures imposed in the name of open and free markets often impose human hardships, such as the painful human and social cost of the IMF reforms in Argentina. Although backed by sound economics, austerity programs enforced by the IMF and other lending organizations can overwhelm some nations. For example, a Standard & Poor's Rating Sheet observed that, "Although much improved, Brazil's debt-servicing ratios remain higher than those of peer credits. Debt service (even excluding short-term debt) as a share of exports of goods and services will still be about 40% in 2005–2006 (down from 97% in 2000)."[6]

Ubiquitous information access can also stir resentment. Poorer populations easily observe what they lack when the wealth of western business and culture is so visibly displayed. As Nayan Chanda, Director of Publications for the Yale Center for the Study of Globalization and winner of Harvard University's 2005 Shorenstein Award for Journalism, noted, "Overt or subliminal political and cultural messages carried with goods, ideas and entertainment from the developed world have added to the sense of disruption in many traditional societies."[7]

Advances are being made, such as the wider recognition of the power of the "Bottom of the Pyramid," a concept conceived by the renowned professor, C.K. Prahalad. He and others like him believe the solution lies in turning the problem of poverty into an opportunity for investment and growth, and through that, enabling those at the bottom of the pyramid to gain access to purchasing power.

This ethos suggests that servicing the poor is not simply an act of doing good, but a powerful way of transforming products and business practices. The innovation required to tailor goods and services to people who earn less than US$2.00 a day can have profound consequences on innovation, quality and efficiency, prompting dramatic improvements in price and performance. Illustrating this point is the example Prahalad offers of the Indian company, Aravind Eye Care.

> "When Aravind Eye Care set out to provide cataract surgery to the poor in southern India, for example, it knew customers could never afford the US$3,000 per procedure that it costs in developed lands. The company devised a system that enables it to provide the surgery for an average of US$25 to US$30 per procedure. Aravind is now the largest eye-care facility on earth; it performs more than 200,000 surgeries a year. Not surprisingly, because of the process innovations it has made, the quality of care Aravind delivers exceeds that of similar surgeries in Britain. Debt-free and highly profitable, Aravind boasts an annual return on equity of more than 75%."[8]

The success of companies like Aravind is inspiring other businesses to follow suit. Local and transnational businesses are starting to investigate and pursue the types of products and services that are in greatest demand in bottom-of-the-pyramid markets. The winners will be those who successfully combine innovation while overcoming distribution and pricing constraints.

This trend should have promising consequences for the competitive environment, both in capturing new markets as well as refining old ones. By creating a means for increased prosperity, these developments also augur well for encouraging peace in the more troubled parts of the world, particularly given the close relationship between economic vigor and political stability. It is in everyone's best interests if private companies, nonprofits, and NGOs continue to work together to create profit-oriented strategies that benefit local producers, employees, and consumers in emerging national markets.

FUTURE EMPIRES: CHANGING CORPORATE—REGIONAL HEGEMONY

The advances that have come with globalization present a formidable competitive asset for those companies that make the best use of them. Whereas established market conditions used to give the edge to large multinational corporations with the scale, purchasing power and muscle to dominate regional markets, their natural supremacy is no longer as assured. Cheap labor from formerly inaccessible markets, such as China, is now available in abundant supply. Capital is also abundant, and at relatively low cost as investors pour their ambitions into promising developing nations.

Expected Annual GDP Growth 2004–2010 (%)	
Leading Developed Countries	
United States	2.25
Western Europe	2.0
Japan	2.0
Emerging High Growth Countries	
China	8.0
Central/Eastern Europe	8.0
Southeast Asia	6.0
India	6.0
Mexico	6.0
Brazil	7.0

Source: Boston Consulting Group[9]

In all, the changes that have come represent a huge shift. The emergence of rapidly developing economies, such as China and India, and aggregated regional markets, create the possibility of real displacement, with old world order, if not pitted, then juxtaposed against the new.

Within this global embrace, the outlines of three controlling economic regions can be discerned. They are the Americas, which include the NAFTA countries of Canada, the United States and Mexico, the expanded European Union, and the emerging power that is the Asia-Pacific region. Most of the world's financial assets are housed within these three regions. In Europe alone, 83% of the financial assets are currently held by just five countries: Germany, the United Kingdom, Italy, Spain and France.

> The populations of China and India represent more than one-third of the world's total population, the vast majority of whom were out of reach to the modern world until recently. Technology has changed that, allowing a fairly spectacular leveraging of labor in a very short space of time.

The increasing share of new market entrants will likely mean that traditional corporate distribution of growth and profits will be less uniform and predictable. In fact, the major developing nations are expected to achieve absolute growth rates that rival that of America, Western Europe and Japan together.

The historical hegemony that has defined the European and American market hold is slowly being challenged. Consider that China now accounts for 5% of total global production. This number may seem small, but not when one recognizes that more than half of this share was earned in just the past five years.

The threat is being felt. U.S. manufacturers are increasingly referring to what they call, "The China Price." *BusinessWeek* called them, "the three scariest words in U.S. Industry."[10] Witness the concern among American textile manufacturers when the quota system implemented by the Uruguay Round Agreement on Textiles and Clothing (ATC) expired in 2005. Chinese prices on average are 30–50% lower than American goods. In other industries, Chinese prices can be lower than the U.S. cost of materials.

It used to be that Europe and America maintained their differentiated position through a chokehold on advanced, knowledge-based industries. In recent years, however, China and its regional neighbors have made strong advances in high-value industries like computing, advanced networking and communications, and sophisticated electronics goods.

Still, the competition is hardly one-sided. Multinationals from Europe and America are beginning to reap large returns from their investments in fast-growing developing nations. A Boston Consulting Group report noted that industrial companies like ABB, Emerson, Schneider Electric and Siemens will generate 5% or more of their total sales from China as early as 2005.[11] In addition, these and other companies have reaped large cost benefits from the massive uptick in outsourcing. With margin pressures rising, they can and have been much more selective about those processes they retain in-house, outsourcing any which can be done faster, better and cheaper somewhere else. In return, their products are far more competitive, both in fast-growing developing markets as well as back home.

Multinationals that fail to recognize the importance of securing a foothold in these new markets may have a hard time making up the competitive advantage of their peers. For most, the emergence of fast-developing economies means the traditional competitive model will undergo a fairly radical transformation. Competing on price is already becoming a zero-sum game for many western companies. However much one downsizes and trims costs, outsources and automates, it is still nearly impossible for Western nations to match Chinese levels. As Oded Shenkar observed in *BusinessWeek*, " 'Shaving 5% here and there won't work.' Chinese producers can make the same adjustments. 'You need an entirely new business model to compete.' "[12]

Given this, what does today's global CEO need to consider when examining the robustness of their business model and its ability to remain vigorous in the global market?

CHALLENGES FACING THE GLOBAL CEO

The core mission of the modern, global CEO remains the same: set a sound strategic direction; retain and recruit the right talent; bring the right processes to bear; and, monitor performance. The new complexity is the business environment surrounding them, one that is shifting and morphing with unprecedented speed. Says Boston Consulting Group, "Today, managers must also be capable of building markets quickly; creating flexible, fast, high performing organizations that are well integrated into the company's global network; managing major facilities; developing a world-class local talent base; and, making strategic decisions with far reaching impacts—not to mention conducting weeklong country tours for steady streams of VIP visitors from headquarters, as well as for customers."[13]

With real-time information updating production and inventory statistics instantly, global companies must constantly tinker with their supply chains to outpace, or even just to keep pace with, their competitors. Such dependency gives supply chain partners greater power than before. Similarly, the hyper-competitive global marketplace is forcing most multinationals to undergo a sweeping organizational transformation. This is one of the most difficult and complex tasks for any CEO and one for which the historical success rates are decidedly mixed. Such massive, cross-continental realignment reduces some aspects of headquarters' control as it empowers the company's regional affiliates.

In light of these altered dynamics, multinational CEOs face five primary challenges:

Visualization

More than ever, CEOs need to be alert to the sources, direction and consequences of change, both in the external marketplace and internally within their own organizations. Benchmarking, scenario planning, competitive analysis, best practice assessments and other tools are all critical for sensing and adapting to fluctuations in the business environment. "Visualization," says Toyota Motor President, Katsuaki Watanabe, "is the key to success."[14] Yet in order to visualize effectively, the organization must be capable of honest self-assessment. Watanabe calls this "Minotake." This climate of fact-based observation and appraisal, he stresses, is critical to helping management distinguish today's organizational realities and needs against the ideal state one is driving toward. Otherwise, Watanabe warns, "Big Company" disease may blind the company from real problems and opportunities.

Talent

Recruiting, retaining and developing the right talent within an organization will become a critical differentiator for global competitiveness. The ability to manage and lead a diverse and increasingly decentralized operating environment will call on non-traditional management skills. The classic line management model will no longer suffice. Rather, the need to groom strategic thinkers will prompt companies to incentivize their 'best and brightest' to serve important career stints in overseas locations as a means of equipping them with the experience of responding to local needs on a global basis. In some companies, foreign secondments are already becoming a requirement for further promotion. Global talent development and mobility, as well as a greater diversity of skill sets, will be vital.

Relationships

While relationships have always been integral to the growth of any business, the quality of relationships for a truly successful global enterprise is paramount. This is because productive relationships are the only means dynamic enough to inform leadership of undulating market changes, customer needs, organizational effectiveness, and ultimately the quality of execution. Maintaining and expanding these types of relationships is an extraordinarily demanding process, usually requiring a long-term investment of time, money and resources. Most multinationals today, particularly those that have grown by acquisition, are facing much needed catch-up in this regard.

Integrated Corporate Culture

Getting a small organization to move and act with one voice is difficult. It is massively complex for companies whose businesses comprise several thousand individuals spread across diverse continents and time zones. Given that the average CEO tenure has shrunk to about five years only adds to the organizational challenge of creating a common corporate culture, as strategic initiatives and leadership styles change. Nonetheless, the most effective global companies will be those whose culture is integrated and unified across their global footprint. Such unity will best facilitate customer advocacy, responsiveness and support and offers the most successful means for the company to leverage its scale. CEOs need to juggle this requirement with a simultaneous need to encourage the development of tailored local market-facing initiatives, to ensure relevance with far-flung and diverse customer needs.

Execution

As Kunio Nakamura, the president of Matsushita, affirmed, "The current business environment is changing every second. You simply cannot afford to lose sight of the slightest changes."[15] In light of this, execution will become paramount in the face of fast-moving competitors and swiftly changing alliances. Even if markets give a nod to long-term investments, they are often harshly unforgiving of short-term errors in execution. More than ever, CEOs will benefit from process improvements, standardized business systems, integrated global functions, and tightly monitored financial and operational controls.

LOOKING AHEAD

Globalization holds the promise of improving the lives of much of the world's population. Since modern globalization emerged in the 1970s, world infant mortality rates have fallen by almost half, adult literacy has increased by one third, and average global lifespan has increased by 11 years. Over the last several decades, the forces of globalization have reduced poverty levels in many countries, but regional differences exist. World Bank statistics show that extreme poverty, those living on less than US$1 a day, decreased 20% from 1981 to 2001. In East Asia, extreme poverty fell from 56% to 16%. Similar gains were made in China and other parts of Asia. Only sub-Saharan Africa suffers the same levels of unabated human misery.

Together, globalization, technology and economic openness are providing unprecedented opportunity, creating an environment that allows for the most efficient manufacturing and distribution of goods and services. These are remarkable changes. Never before in history have so many natural barriers to border-free commerce been removed.

According to the World Bank, three billion people in 24 emerging nations were integrated into the world economy over the past two decades. These economies achieved higher growth in per capita income (5% compared to 2% in developed economies), longer life expectancy, better education and diminished poverty. *Source: WEF Annual Meeting 2005, Strategic Insight Report*

For business leaders, the promise of globalization lies in building enduring businesses. Simply put, to win in the global arena requires business men and women to:

❑ Take responsibility for developing a world in which the benefits of growth are broadly shared, in which globalization means rising incomes and opportunity for all people.

❑ Recognize that one's best competitive opportunities arise when healthy competitive markets are available to all.

❑ Recommit their organizations to an international agenda of free markets, free trade, and free democratic choice.

❑ Conduct business on the basis of uncompromising ethical values.

Going forward, the mission statement of many dynamic global companies will be more multi-faceted than at present. The end game is to increase value and profitability, to leverage each nation or region's competitive advantage and to deepen international collaboration.

CHAPTER 2

A New Equation
for Success

*"We, in business, do have a calling. We have a calling to reward
the confidence of those who have hired us and to build something
lasting and good in the process."*

**—Roberto C. Goizueta,
former chairman and CEO, Coca-Cola Company**

The classic equation for doing business remains: deliver
the right product in the right place for the right price at
the right time. In today's global market, this means that a
truck sold in Toronto may have been assembled in Mexico
from parts manufactured in Korea with a price negotiated
over the Internet.

As business models undulate in response, we look at
whether or not size matters. We examine the comparative advantages of large companies over a newer breed of global
competitor. In response to the volatility of the emerging competitive landscape, we consider seven fundamental character-

istics that informed leaders can use to build and guide enduring businesses.

DAVID AND GOLIATH: THE COMPARATIVE ADVANTAGE OF SIZE AND SCALE

James B. Lee, Jr., Vice Chairman of J.P. Morgan Chase, put it this way to *Institutional Investor*, "Bigger is not better. Bigger is absolutely mandatory." In the race to secure an enduring foothold in both emerging and domestic markets, the top seeded runners have been blue-chip businesses with large market capitalizations, well-known brands, and a wide network of international operations. Without a diversified portfolio of market leading products, the financial leverage to negotiate with suppliers or the reach to tap far flung markets around the world, competitor incursions can be more damaging. Large, high-performance companies benefit from a lower cost of capital and cheaper procurement costs, better credit terms, superior negotiating muscle, as well as, importantly, an ability to attract and retain superior talent.

> *UNCTAD*
>
> The United Nations Conference on Trade and Development (UNCTAD) reports that "twenty-nine of the world's 100 largest economic entities (by which the UN includes nation-states) are transnational corporations." *Source: UNCTAD, 2002*

The flexibility that size affords a multinational is a major competitive advantage if for no other reason than it gives established businesses greater permission to experiment and a greater cushion against failure. Whereas a smaller company may be compelled by necessity to focus on one product line or area of research, a large global company with a portfolio of market leading products can spread its risk broadly.

Proven cash cows generate revenue that can be funneled into research and a number of new product lines, while also providing plenty of cover. Some test lines may fail, but others may generate huge returns. This dexterity helps blue chip companies address high degrees of product complexity and deal with supply chain issues that span geographies and functions.

Additionally, in response to ever-pressing time-to-market issues, a large and diversified company can boast a fatter pipeline, permitting greater control over the product lifecycle. They can structure release flow to adapt to shorter product shelf lives and manage inventory and obsolescence issues with improved predictability.

Employee Satisfaction

Analysis of employee satisfaction by the Business Research Lab indicates that employers with 500 or more employees were on average less satisfied with their jobs than companies with fewer than 100 employees.

The naturally larger stride that big companies have is equally valuable from a competitive standpoint. Although a new entrant may leverage a customer pleasing innovation to take a market leading position, the lead, itself, is often temporary as large companies find it proportionally easier to catch up. Microsoft has proven this time and again. Although slower to market with the Internet and certain other innovations, Microsoft recovered quickly, using their massive financial and marketing muscle to overtake smaller rivals.

Large companies also have the ear of powerful people in a way that smaller companies plainly do not. They wield not only huge economic power, but immense political influence around the globe. High quality relationships in circles of power provide access and stature. Together, buying power, global reach, deep resources, and the breadth to experiment puts large companies in a strong position to carve out a global advantage. It is a good place to be.

Therefore, it can be surprising to witness turbulence at the top. As we shall see, size is no guarantee of long-term success.

CHINKS IN THE ARMOR

The Fortune 500 is one of the most respected corporate rankings in the world. With even the 500th company on the list pulling in revenues over US$3 billion, inclusion is evidence of massive size and scale. The global list includes such corporate giants as Hewlett-Packard, GE, Microsoft, Toyota, Wal-Mart and their peers. Getting on the list is a tremendous achievement. So is staying on it.

Of the nearly 2000 companies that have appeared on the Fortune 500 list since its inception in 1955, only 71 have consistently remained on the list, year-in and year-out, since then.

Long Lineage

Some of the oldest, continually operating companies on the Fortune
500 include: Bank of New York, founded in 1784; Cigna, formerly the
Insurance Company of North America, founded in 1792; State Street
Corp, formerly Union Bank, founded in 1792; and Dominion Resources, formerly the Upper Appomattox Company, founded in
1795. *Source: Fortune Magazine*

This churn among what would appear to be the most stable
of the world's corporate demographic is notable. After all,
these are industry's titans. Most are already at least 40 years
old and have weathered a great manner of economic and
competitive disruptions, from war and social transformation
to years of great technological upheaval.[16] If, as schooled, one
is looking for a sound, long-term investment, most of these
companies would seem a conservative bet. And, of course,
many have and continue to reward their shareholders amply.

Still, consider this. It has only been 51 years since the in-
augural Fortune 500 list was published in 1955. However, of
the top 20 companies then reported, only seven remain today.
As Geoff Colvin, a columnist and reporter for *Wall $treet Week
with Fortune* noted, "You would have surveyed the top 20
companies with a feeling of comfort and confidence that
these stalwart enterprises would proceed majestically into the
future as far as the eye could see. But of course they didn't.
U.S. Steel was No. 3; today it's a small-cap value stock.
Chrysler was No. 6; now it's part of DaimlerChrysler, a German company. Bethlehem Steel was No. 12; last year it finally
disappeared completely."

The topple rate from lists such as the Fortune 500 has accelerated in recent times. The French business school, *INSEAD*, determined that the failure rate of companies was four times higher in the 1990s than in the 1970s. As pressure from mounting global competition has grown, so has volatility. By the mid 1980s, one-third of the companies listed in the Fortune 500 in 1970 had been acquired, broken up or were no longer in business. Today, that figure has grown to a staggering 60%. The quickening turnover has been catalyzed in part by the economic downturn and the subsequent wave of merger and acquisition activity across industry. It has also been triggered by new and rising forms of competition.

OLD VERSUS NEW

The organizational structure of long-established, mature businesses can yield desirable benefits in the form of improved consistency, efficiency and accuracy. Its hierarchical nature also facilitates succession. However, while mature industries can excel at bringing cohesion, order and process to

Size Limits

"In recent years, the defense that business must be large to enjoy economies of large-scale production has faded in importance. The argument lost force as it became increasingly apparent that the size of our modern corporate giants is far beyond any conceivable requirements of efficiency. Furthermore, there is evidence that, in some industries, the trend of technology has reversed itself and is now reducing the size of plant required for efficient operation." *Estes Kefauver, U.S. Senator, 1965* diverse streams of activity, they can be slow to accept and respond to change. Wired for consistency, long-standing entities can suffer from decision making processes that are backward looking and incremental.

Wittingly or not, such cultures can stymie out-of-the-box thinking. Innovators can be perceived as "not playing the game." Competitive threats can go unrecognized. As such, old-line companies may be vulnerable to a new breed of global competitor, many of which are rising rapidly from emerging developing economies. Katsuaki Watanabe, the president of Toyota Motor Corporation, warned "We must remember that an organization has a tendency to multiply itself."[17] At Toyota, Watanabe consciously tries to streamline the company's business processes continuously to maintain its competitive advantage.

Leveraging open-market reforms, sophisticated companies in rapidly developing economies can extend their reach to customers around the world. Since technology is size-neutral, these players can adapt quickly to provide customers with flexible and customized products. Cheap and abundant labor and the growing manufacturing infrastructure found in many rapidly developing countries offer new local market players strong tools for growth.

Together, these business drivers are molding the underlying economic basis of doing business. Recognizing that size does count, markets are aggregating. Regional industrial zones are forming in many parts of the world with business communities coming together to form virtual supply chains and trading partnerships. Brain trusts such as those that have defined Silicon Valley are springing up in many industrial corridors in India and beyond, providing a catalyst for creative ventures and innovation, spurring fast execution. These dynamics, combined with the leveling effect that is technology, help narrow the size advantage of larger competitors and enable emerging companies to achieve scale of their own.

The laws of economics dictate that the lower the barrier to entry, the greater the number of competitors. As globalization brings new regions into the world's marketplace, small, aggressive and flexible start-ups will be on the increase. Over time, their numbers may steadily chip away at larger company market share. Still, small companies have their work cut out for them. While mature industries may face the threat of more intense competition and stiffer growth hurdles, small organizations endure the challenges of raising needed capital, handling rapid growth and accessing the right talent and resources. Nonetheless, as they refine their business models, regional players will increasingly offer buyers an efficient purchasing option and a compelling value proposition.

Large or small, a diversified global footprint, world-scale volume and established global brand are critical for ongoing success. As today's leaders respond to a host of pressing business concerns, uppermost is the need to build a secure foundation for growth. With the average lifespan of companies shrinking—tested by unprecedented forms of competition—what are the best doing to build enduring businesses and steer their employees and stakeholders through the swells of change?

SEVEN CHARACTERISTICS OF ENDURING BUSINESSES

Profits, return on equity, and market capitalization are strong indicators of current health, but they are not, as we have seen, predictors of long-term survival. As entities design their future, they will retrain their focus to look outside, recalibrate their organizational structure to be more responsive, and rethink their methods for encouraging innovation in a bid to provide superior resiliency and agility.

From our conversations and experience with global leaders, as well as our own research into those factors most critical to long-term success, we have developed the following seven characteristics. We hope they provide valuable context for today's leaders in designing and thinking about their own corporate blueprint.

I. Change from the Outside-In

Change from within is often espoused as an optimum means of transforming an organization. Yet, in a period of rapid market evolution, inward-focusing ideologies create a competitive drag. By contrast, those organizations whose eyes are trained to observe outward changes in their industry, geography and peer group can more quickly turn and adapt their organization. As management guru Peter Drucker states, taking a less inward focus compels a firm to become more intelligent about customers, both current and potential ones. The discomfort in adopting such an approach is that it is inherently messier. When the priority is given to understanding external economic and structural forces, internal processes will be subject to more frequent change. In response, procedures for internal reporting and strategy development must become less static. Effective leadership communication will become essential for coordinating directives to outward facing teams. The successful organization of the future will be molded by timely knowledge about the global marketplace. First mover advantage will go to those companies that can make the most real-time adaptations in response.

Kunio Nakamura, the president of Matsushita, ensures his company stays responsive to outside changes.[18] He has structured his company to be flat, and, as he puts it, "web-like" with very strong and continuously enhanced IT that is essential to his business serving as the heart of his company's infrastructure and innovations. Nakamura chose this type of structure precisely because it "provides us capabilities to be working alongside customers around the world." Now, he states, "When the pace of change accelerates, we respond." He adds that he is committed to transforming his management model from what he calls the "lead-ball type" that is heavily loaded into a "soccer-ball type" of management that is lightly loaded and far more outwardly directed toward the company's customers.

II. Create a Performance Meritocracy

Enduring companies are ruthless about excellence. They pay extraordinary attention to the quality of their people, as well as to training, growing and motivating core talent. People are the defining asset in the knowledge economy. Because of this, the productivity and innovation demands spurred by radical competition leave no room for mediocrity. Employees that have competency in more than one functional area, language mastery in more than one tongue, and service experience in one or more foreign posts will be at a premium.

They will also be expected to exhibit exceptional commitment. To paraphrase an old saying, those from whom much is demanded, much must be given. High-quality employees in most industries are already working record numbers of hours. Downsizing, mergers and other business changes have left modern workers feeling less company loyalty than in past generations. To retain and grow valued talent, global managers will need to confront these issues swiftly and, in some cases, boldly.

Ultimately, companies and star employees alike benefit from a clearly articulated employee value proposition, one that is developed with the same thought and analysis as a corporate value proposition.[19] This means that not only do the traditional human resource parameters come into play, but other motivational drivers as well. A study by the Wharton School of Business found that employees felt most positive about their jobs when the assigned tasks delivered a tangible sense of achievement, i.e., there was a fixed beginning and an end.[20] Other studies have shown that achievement, recognition and a strong sense of internal community go furthest in motivating employees, keeping them challenged and retaining them down the road.

Although Chapter Three delves into global talent issues more comprehensively, it is important to state here, from the point of view of sustaining success, that effective employee recruiting, development and retention starts at the top. Effective leaders will exert creativity in forging meaningful career paths for key talent and will be more exacting in trimming resources that do not fit or perform to the heightened standards of the global marketplace.

III. Remove Internal Boundaries

Turf-wars and the "not-invented-here" syndrome are common ailments in many established businesses. Despite efforts to encourage teaming across disciplines, many organizations still suffer from stove-piped structures. Heavily matrixed or silo-based activity can suppress creative exchange. In the past, however, these structures did not overly handicap performance. That is changing. In the age of radical competition, agility is at a premium. Companies that can quickly form and disband collaborative teams comprising subject matter specialists from across their enterprise will have a distinct advantage over more structurally hidebound peers.

The best companies are responding. In order to elicit the right behaviors from their teams, smart leaders are revisiting their management training programs, requiring rising stars to serve periods in diverse functions and/or geographies in order to ascend to positions of upper management. Those who make genuine efforts to remove internal boundaries will receive superior career advancement over others who are slower to change or encourage cross-collaboration.

GE's John F. Welch Leadership Center was the world's first major corporate business school. Its mission is to create, identify and transfer organizational learning to enhance GE's competitiveness worldwide. Today it is recognized as one of the world's foremost leadership training programs and a breeding ground for future CEOs.

Jack Welch took this notion to heart upon assuming the mantle of General Electric many years ago. GE then, as now, was a massive operation with dozens of discrete businesses. Back then, however, the company's performance was uneven. Some divisions excelled. Others underperformed. While lack of strategic focus was partially to blame, Welch saw that an equally significant problem was the divisional rivalries that existed within his various business units.

In response, Welch made the creation of a boundary less organization a top-down leadership objective.[21] He instructed direct reports to eradicate their silo culture and made sure that employees were given incentives to work collaboratively. The resulting combination of discipline, focus and teaming sharply transformed GE's productivity levels. Today GE invests about US$1 billion annually on training and education programs, from assembly lines, to corporate classrooms, to boardrooms, and is consistently ranked as one of the most admired companies in the world.

IV. Foster Autonomous Innovation

In their landmark innovation study, *The Sources of Invention*, British scholars John Jewkes, David Sawers and Richard Stillerman, researched 61 of the most important inventions of the twentieth century, everything from the ball-point pen and the zipper to penicillin and the jet engine. What they learned was that most of the world's creative discoveries came from individuals working as sole inventors or in small research laboratories, and not from the research and development wings of large companies.[22] The jet engine was pioneered through its early stages by two individual inventors, an Englishman and a German working virtually simultaneously, each unbeknownst to the other. Neither had any connection to the aircraft industry and neither was an engine specialist. Similarly, most of the basic inventions for radio were delivered by individual inventors with no relation to communications businesses.[23]

Built for Optimization

"While there will always be advantages to size and scope . . . the industrial company was built for optimization, not innovation." Gary Hamel, chairman of the consulting firm Strategos. *Source: Fast Company*

Indeed, as long-time management consultant Tom Peters, put it, "Innovation does not occur where it is supposed to." He suggests that big companies have a poor record of innovation compared to small company rivals. Richard Foster, author of *Innovation: The Attacker's Advantage*, agrees. "Big firms," he writes, "stick too long with today's winners. If they are to have a chance at continued vitality, they must abandon the skills and products that have brought them success." The stumbling block, Foster argues, is that big companies are too often inclined to rely on financial models that urge managers to over-fund incremental improvements in successful products while downplaying less predictable, but potentially more profitable future products.[24]

Other management scholars, such as Clayton Christiansen, author of *Disruptive Innovation*, suggest that it is sometimes easier for innovation to flourish outside the boundaries of large companies. This is how Flarion Technologies began. In 2000, a bright engineer named Rajiv Laroia at Lucent Technologies' Bell Laboratories division was tasked with leading a team to improve wireless standards for transmitting data. In the course of their development, this team came upon a radically new way to deliver data that was faster and cheaper than the company's existing system. The problem was that Lucent, which had a significant investment in its then current technologies, was hesitant to adopt the new approach.

Valuing Discomfort

"If you are comfortable, all you are doing is making yourself a target." *Source: Intelligent Enterprise Magazine*

As Laroia recounted in an interview with *Fast Company* magazine, "It's not easy for large companies to cannibalize their own products." Frustrated, Laroia and his team left Lucent to found Flarion. Although still a startup, the company's broadband solutions have been popular with brand-name clients like Nextel, T-Mobile, Siemens and others. Today Flarion has offices in the U.S., London, Tokyo, Sydney and Singapore.[25]

This does not mean that giants are prohibited from realizing the benefits of thriving entrepreneurship and invention. Recognizing, as Peters states, "that the presence of a swarm of small start-ups is an unparalleled stimulant to the clumsy behemoths," the behemoths themselves can do much to foster productive incubator relationships in promising technologies.

Some are creating cluster groups or "constellations" of innovation, providing direct equity into, or forging strong, supportive partnerships, with an amalgam of university and start-up research groups. Most models bring together academics, entrepreneurs and engineers. Together, they experiment with out-of-the-ordinary ideas that can be transformed into startup companies with seed money.

BMW Group leverages the best of both worlds, building a strong internal innovation capability and coupling that with ties to the external scientific community. With the motto "Passion for Innovation," the BMW Group delivers on its brand promise through its "innovation network." The nucleus of this brain trust lies in the BMW Group's renowned Research and Innovation Center, known by its German abbreviation, FIZ. The FIZ in turn connects four satellite innovation centers in Germany, Austria, Japan and the United States. Anchored by this internal research collaboration, BMW Group hones innovation further by reaching beyond its borders to the external scientific community. The group is active in conducting joint projects with many universities and research institutes. It also sponsors the internationally recognized "Scientific Award," one that, true to BMW's belief in the power of networks, recognizes outstanding student achievement through the interdisciplinary approach to scientific experimentation. BMW Group CFO Stefan Krause believes such ties are critical. He states, "they allow us to keep our finger on the pulse of all markets in order to recognize trends early and respond rapidly."

Other companies catalyze innovation by funding in-house venture-capital divisions. Intel Capital, the strategic investment arm of semiconductor leader, Intel Corporation, is one of the oldest, largest and most successful global corporate venture programs. It is also the primary driver of Intel's internal new business incubation. Since its founding in 1991, Intel's in-house VC unit has invested more than US$4 billion in roughly 1,000 companies across 30 countries.

Under the leadership of Arvind Sodhani, president of Intel Capital, the investment team tracks global innovators whose business models align with the strategic and financial aims of Intel Corporation. Said Sodhani, "We work with our portfolio companies to establish new and innovative technologies, develop industry standard solutions, drive global Internet growth, enable new usage models, and advance the computing and communications platforms."[26]

Such focus allows Intel, the parent, tremendous dexterity when it comes to incubating innovation. Not only can the company tap promising technologies for its own use, it can also, through its investment portfolio companies, create what Sodhani calls, "separate ecosystems," that bring a different but valuable set of additional benefits to Intel.

Whatever method a company chooses to incubate the leading solutions of tomorrow must be flexible enough to accommodate the frequently chaotic and undisciplined process of innovation. As we all know, innovation does not conform neatly to conventional and orderly business management. By recognizing these inherent qualities and fostering a culture that shepherds specialized innovation both inside and outside the four main walls of the business, large and small companies alike can prosper.

V. Know Your Markets

One might think Nestlé and Unilever, two extraordinarily large and successful businesses, would have little difficulty breaking into almost any foreign market. After all, Unilever N.V. is one of the world's largest producers of packaged goods, with operations in virtually every country in North America, Europe, Asia, Africa, the Middle East and Latin America. Similarly, Nestlé, as the number one food processor, has vast institutional experience competing in diverse regions of the globe.

Nonetheless, as David Arnold, a former professor of marketing at Harvard Business School discovered, they did struggle at first. His book, *The Mirage of Global Markets*, details the story of Unilever's and Nestlé's initial foray into the Saudi ice cream marketplace. In preparation for their respective product launches, both companies conducted market research and prepared detailed business plans.

The problem was not planning. Instead, the new lines' undoing came from certain unique societal issues in Saudi Arabia of which the companies were initially unaware. For one thing Saudis, unlike Westerners, consider ice cream as a snack, not as a dessert to be purchased and consumed at home. For another, women in Saudi Arabia do not generally hold driver's licenses. Since the ice cream was primarily sold through supermarkets, women, the targeted demographic, were not often in a position to buy it.

Over time, the two companies recognized and corrected their market approach. Today, both hold dominant market share positions in Saudi Arabia. Yet, the story highlights the fact that size alone, while indicative of success, will only sustain it when the tastes and customs of local markets are factored into the company's equation.

Contrast Nestlé's and Unilever's market lesson in the Arabian Peninsula against that of Citibank's experience in Bangalore, India. Because a higher than average percentage of Bangalore's population lives in relative poverty, Citibank recognized that many potential customers would be prevented from participating in the bank's customary checking products. Rather than let the market go untapped, Citibank tailored something new. The resulting product, called Suvidha, is distinguished by its low deposit limit of US$25.

To Citibank's surprise, pent up demand among Bangaloreans for reliable financial services was much stronger than expected. During its first year of launch, Suvidha secured over 150,000 new accounts. The reaction from the public was extraordinary. Citibank's innovation and local market sensitivity spurred strong positive bottom line results.

Today, the bank continues to evolve Suvidha. In response to high rates of local illiteracy, Citibank is testing various types of graphical imagery as proxies for the written word.[27] Suvidha is now seen as a model for peer banks to emulate in similar underserved markets.

These stories illustrate the profound impact local market sensitivities can have on business economics. Investing time in understanding the specific needs of local and regional markets can reward both customers and shareholders alike.

VI. Test Assumptions and Execute with Discipline

Strong companies recognize that financial rigor and discipline are the backbone to growth. People and corporations are naturally optimistic. You believe your business has strong potential, otherwise why invest the time, resources and energy. This optimism engenders passion and drive, but can occasionally blind leaders from hard facts. It takes a dispassionate leader to challenge the available data.

Sophisticated organizations appreciate this and instill rigorous controls to govern critical processes. Their leaders distinguish between cost effectiveness and competitive effectiveness. In doing so, they enable thoughtful strategy and careful decision-making over such things as when it is optimal to invest in world-scale plants and when it is best to offshore certain activities. Budgeting and capital expenditures are oriented around the company's competitive blueprint and based on the company's ability to respond quickly to competitor movements in key markets. It is in this fashion that mature companies can exercise the twin ideals of fiscal discipline and a culture of innovation.

Mature businesses are by definition often viewed as slow growth. Roberto Goizueta, chairman and CEO of Coca-Cola from 1981 until his death in 1997, proved otherwise. In studying Goizueta's legacy, management adviser, Ram Charan, noted that Goizueta's dictum was to attend to the core business and always take an unblemished view of the facts.

While many considered Pepsi to be Coca-Cola's primary adversary, Goizueta took a different view. He instructed his management team to look at Coke's actual universe of competitors, namely all ingestible liquids. This pitted Coke against whatever else went into a customer's stomach. Instead of carbonated beverage, water emerged as the chief rival. "By this definition," Charan noted, "Coke's 40%-plus market share became 3%, changing the company's view of growth."

This altered perspective reconfigured Coke's marketing practices. Goizueta's discipline to stick to the facts and reassess the competitive landscape caused Coke to change in other ways too, from redesigned processes to a shift in its international positioning. The "mature" company responded well. All told, Charan noted that by 1997 Goizueta "pushed Coke's overseas profits up to nearly 80% of total earnings."[28]

For companies to clearly see the facts depends on their competitive intelligence capabilities. While most businesses perform some benchmarking, and nearly all compare industry statistics, not many invest in active programs that examine rival practices among existing competitors. Fewer still dedicate resources to studying emerging, but still nascent, market trends.

The rising competitive regions of Asia and Latin America can make this challenge more pressing. It's not unusual for a leading executive of a promising Asian company to receive formal educational or professional training in the United States and Europe. It's much less common for the inverse to occur. While China is being panned like a modern gold rush by corporations from all geographies, its customs, language, practices and businesses are much less well known on average to American and European managers. This can make it harder for them to discern small-scale trends that could have a potentially large impact down the road. Training regional managers and field staff to observe and report on changes of this nature might arm corporate leadership with raw data from which to spot and respond to larger changes in market direction.

VII. Acquire Success

Acquisitions will remain a compelling vehicle through which corporations can build enduring businesses and retain their innovation lead. The most successful use deal flow as a means of sustaining their comparative size, scale and product advantage.

Conventional wisdom holds that the majority of mergers and acquisitions fail to create shareholder value. Indeed, the

3M

A company like 3M, which makes everything from masking tape to asthma inhalers, appreciates sound integration discipline. A global corporation whose non-U.S. sales account for more than half of overall revenues, 3M relies on mergers and acquisitions (M&A) to protect and grow its competitive position. Recognizing that successfully integrating a deal can be an Achilles heel, 3M appoints a full-time integration manager to each one transaction. Their role is to oversee a detailed methodology comprising 2,000 steps. The result? Since instituting the changes, 3M has sped deal integration by 81%. *Source: KPMG LLP (U.S.) M&A Share Forum, Oct 2004*

demise of the AOL-Time Warner merger and other prominent Internet era deals often serve as evidence supporting this viewpoint. However, alliances, licenses and acquisitions are, and will remain, an important business tool. Those who approach them carefully can achieve competitive differentiation, especially against less established businesses that have to build partnerships from scratch.

The key, of course, is executing deals well. Robert F. Bruner, the respected University of Virginia Business School professor, studied the conventional wisdom on M&A. His research, which focused on value creation, revealed that the transactions that generated the most tangible value for both targets and buyers displayed a few key characteristics:

o   The buyer and seller were in closely related industries.
o   The industries were not in "hot," and thus possibly inflated, sectors.
o   The buyer was in a position of health and looking to transform the target rather than the other way around.[29]

Well-executed transactions are an important means of attracting top management and other talent. They deliver tactical assistance by paring operations costs and minimizing overcapacity. Companies can use mergers to control both a product and its distribution—the pattern for many recent media mergers. Others use the transaction to broaden the range of what they sell, as in many financial service sector deals.

Revenue growth is one reason behind the current wave of merger activity. In an era of low inflation, companies are challenged to raise prices in an effort to have customers pay more. That means revenue growth is dependent upon increasing the number of products or units sold, which can be difficult to achieve in large, established industries. The pursuit of ever-narrowing margins and product innovations will likely make mergers and acquisitions and other types of business combinations a permanent tool for those looking to maintain a market leading presence.

CONCLUSION

What keeps GE managers up at night? Can anyone really threaten Wal-Mart? While a serious challenge to their current dominance is unlikely in the short term, the same might have been said about McDonald's in 1971. That's when Dave Thomas decided to challenge the hamburger chain's juggernaut. At the time, people thought he was crazy. After all, what was he thinking—take on McDonald's, the industry's giant, with thousands of franchisees and a quarter-pounder in nearly every zip code? But that's just what Thomas did. He differentiated his product by shaping hamburgers into squares, out of respect for his beloved grandmother who told him never to cut corners, and was the first to introduce significant innovations to the typical burger chain menu. Three decades later, Wendy's is among the largest franchisors in the world. Their share price growth has exceeded McDonald's over the past five years.

The point is this: as companies seek to define and build new dimensions of value, the seven characteristics described will differentiate those who endure from those whose tenure is more transient. Implicit in this is a lesson about how we think about change. For all that is said about market turbulence, companies can thrive and prosper in the face of immense change. Those who do, will build markets quickly, create nimble, flexible, high-performing organizations, develop a world-class local talent base, and make strategic decisions with far-reaching impacts.

CHAPTER 3

A Simple Vision for Complex Times

"The most successful companies and the most successful countries will be those that manage human capital in the most effective fashion."

—Gary S. Becker, Nobel Prize winning economist who coined the phrase "human capital."

Far-sighted companies are focusing on wider dimensions of value as they seek to fulfill their responsibilities to the communities in which they operate. This desire is fueled by a common sense realization that what is good for key stakeholders generates long-term benefits for the business itself.

And what is good for stakeholders in this era of radical competition comes down to a very simple proposition: to be the best, you need to attract and retain the best. Simply put, the most enduring global businesses will be those that stand out as an employer of choice for the most talented and driven individuals in their industry.

STEMMING THE TIDE

Companies have long been intent on recruiting the "best and the brightest." But the challenges in doing so are getting steeper. While some employees do spend their entire career in the service of one employer, the majority do not. Indeed, average employee tenure is shrinking. Surveys in Canada, Australia, New Zealand and some European countries indicate that employee tenure has fallen from an average of 10 years during the 1980s to less than five years today. In the United States, that number is even lower. The U.S. National Employee Relationship Report stated that American employees spend an average of 3.6 years with a company before making their departure.

The issues surrounding global competitiveness add to the challenge. The international marketplace is huge, while talented, knowledgeable workers remain in high demand. Although unemployment levels are a concern in some parts of the world, in the rapidly growing Asian economies, companies are scrambling to fill an escalating need for well-qualified professionals. In IT outsourcing hot-beds like India, the outsourcers themselves are facing unprecedented turnover levels, as high as one-third annually in some companies, as good employees seek better offers and opportunities elsewhere, sometimes at competing entities.

While there will always be an irreducible minimum of turnover in key talent, "brain drain" is a competitive issue. Stanford Business School professor and organizational behavior expert Jeffrey Pfeffer acknowledges that, "Compelling evidence suggests that organizational success comes more from managing people effectively than from attaining large size, operating in a high-growth industry, or becoming lean and mean through downsizing. . ."[30]

The economic need to streamline costs and improve process efficiency is a necessary focus for all businesses. Yet, downsizing, mergers, acquisitions and other business disruptions have hurt some employee/employer relationships. In an era when the public perception of the business community and corporate behavior is low, when skepticism over corporate motives and integrity is high, and when cynicism among employees abounds, it is more incumbent than ever for forward-thinking leaders to rediscover what the corporation is sincerely passionate about: its purpose and its people.

As Richard Bahner, former global human resources director for AT&T once said, "If you look at what management must do it really boils down to three things. Finance: that's yesterday's newspaper. By the time it hits the books, it's too late to do anything about it. Legal: that's today, that's staying straight within the law. But human resource management: that's the future. Employees who can take in a broad scan of information and know enough about their marketplace to integrate that information into new products and services have tremendous abilities to leverage the company's success around the world."[31]

WORK TO LIVE

Work-life balance is an important concept for all companies who desire to become an Employer of Choice. Far from being the "soft" issue it once was considered, work-life issues are now recognized as a matter of competitive business sense. To the best companies go the best employees. It's as simple as that.

An Employer of Choice program is a deliberate corporate-wide recruitment and retention strategy designed to incorporate work-life issues into the fiber of the company's culture. The recognition that strong Employer of Choice companies receive enhances the organization's brand, which, in turn, usually improves sales. It is no surprise that strong Employer of Choice companies usually lead peers in profitability and performance.

For Home Depot, one such company, being an Employer of Choice means, "Leveraging associates' happiness to make them more productive, more loyal and more valuable contributors."[32]

The backbone of Home Depot's Employer of Choice policy lies in seven tenets:

1. Fostering an inclusive and associate-centered culture.
2. Providing meaningful and challenging work.
3. Developing people to realize their potential.
4. Creating opportunity for growth and development.
5. Recognizing contributions and rewarding achievement.
6. Offering frequent, open and two-way communications.
7. Providing economic opportunity through exceptional benefits packages to full-time and part-time associates.[33]

In order to realize its goals, Home Depot holds individual store-by-store Employer of Choice forums, in which employees have the opportunity to communicate career and workplace issues directly to district and regional managers. Though in its early stages, the forums have received generally strong reaction from employees, many of whom call it a positive development and are impressed that management is taking Employer of Choice and their input seriously.

Creating an Employer of Choice initiative requires that leadership and human resource management first create a positioning plan that plots desired gains in employee satisfaction across a range of performance and cultural metrics. Second, whether through surveys, focus groups or other instruments, there needs to be a formalized method for collecting input from staff and external target markets. Third, and perhaps most importantly, the company must then put in place a series of communications and response mechanisms that inform employees about the company's commitment to creating an Employer of Choice environment and what that means for them. Finally, as with all strategies, the company should provide periodic evaluation against objectives and elicit feedback from employees in order to continually improve and tailor the program as the company grows.

One of the most important drivers behind Employer of Choice initiatives is the critical nature of work-life balance. This can include flexible or alternative work schedules, on-site child care, family and compassionate leave, and similar programs. Empowering the employee to fit work into the construct of their life, rather than squeezing life into the confines of their work, ultimately creates a happier and more productive workforce.

When an employee at a large financial services firm learned his spouse had cancer, he was in a quandary. There was no way that his accrued vacation time would cover the amount needed to stay home and care for his wife and two children while she was undergoing treatment. Sensing the concern, the employee's supervisor spread the word to his managers and co-workers. The response was overwhelming. Enough vacation hours were donated from the vacation accounts of individual employees and management to provide for more than 12 months of leave, far more than the employee needed. After the fortunate recovery of his spouse, the employee returned to work deeply grateful for his company's support and with stronger loyalty and goodwill toward his manager and co-workers. The Employer of Choice outreach benefited everyone, including the company itself.

In England, the London borough of Merton Council was suffering from weak employee morale, high rates of absenteeism and staff turnover. As part of a pilot program, the Council introduced a flexible and alternative work program that allowed employees to compress their workweek or work from home. The results surprised even the program's architects. Over the course of the pilot, absenteeism dropped by 50% and productivity rose by 30%.[34] The Council's flexible work-life program is now being used as a best practice in other councils throughout England.

While work/life balance is a critical component of workplace harmony and employee retention, satisfied employees are motivated by several factors, including challenging work, solid career prospects, fair compensation and a supportive work environment. Although employees leave their jobs for a variety of reasons, the opportunity for more rewarding career development usually tops the list in most surveys.[35]

Visionary leaders of outstanding global corporations recognize that the organizations that are best able to create a culture that fosters meaning and purpose for its employees will be much harder to defeat.

A person experiences labor as rewarding when the work itself is aligned with their personal values and when the mission of their company embodies principles with which they strongly identify. In this context, the CEO is the architect of organizational values.

People want to be part of an organization that provides them with personal fulfillment. According to Harvard Business School scholars Joel M. Podolny, Rakesh Khurana and Marya Hill-Popper, one of the most important leadership responsibilities is the creation of a shared ideal for employees and stakeholders alike. In an interview with *HBS Working Knowledge*, they stated:

> "Organizations, like individuals, search for stability and meaning. This search often ends when organizations identify a set of morally sustaining ideals. Ideals animate and help direct decision making in an organization or a society. . . We all recognize that compromise is an essential part of organizational life, but ideals create aspirations for an organization's members."[36]

There are two important aspects to job satisfaction. One is the quality of the work. The other is the quality of the employee's working relationships. These not only include internal, co-worker relationships, but also those with the outside community. To the extent that employees can imbue their work with traces of their own values and ideas, their jobs will become more rewarding. Work/life issues subside when the divide between them becomes less distinguishable. To that end, scholars such as Podolny, Khurana and Popper suggest that among the ways sophisticated companies can invest meaning in the workplace and engage employees for the long-term are to give them a cause:

❑ That they care about.
❑ That is extremely challenging.
❑ That they can personally shape and direct.
❑ That has well-defined milestones.
❑ That, done well, will deliver tangible benefits to the company, the community and/or the employee directly.

A GROWTH CULTURE—FOR BUSINESS AND EMPLOYEE

Businesses that tailor a professional development plan for core employees, as opposed to simply an annual performance review, might receive uplift in retention. By harnessing untapped motivation and loyalty, these companies may also gain an incremental difference in performance and productivity. Together, they may carve out just enough differentiation to stake out, defend, and even expand a market leading position.

The annual performance appraisal process is the traditional means used to tailor employee aspirations with performance expectations. Though often well-designed and well-intentioned, goal setting and appraisal practices tend to be static, short-term minded and not typically designed to handle the constantly shifting responsibilities assigned to an employee during the course of a year. Equally important, they may have only a subjective correlation between work done and reward received.

A major study by the Career Innovation Research center, based in the UK, involving 1,000 young "high-flyers" from 73 nations found that 40% intended to leave their present job within two years. This shorter-term mentality, the study found, was driven in large part by a desire among young talented professionals to increase their professional development, employability and financial rewards.[37] Because many companies lack formal career development programs, employees created their own tracks by job-hopping to obtain desired experience. Conversely, employees who receive regular career development attention are more likely to stay in their jobs.

This speaks not only to the value of long-term mentorship, but also to the importance of the personal business relationship. The following excerpt from *The China Business Review* captures this aspect well:

> '"The personal relationship of the manager and employee is very important. The sense of loyalty is to the person—the

company is nothing, it's a building. You need to move beyond work, to family. You have to invest some time in getting to know your employees." This opinion was echoed by another HR executive who noted, "Superiors are very important. Most people leave companies because they lose confidence or interest in their boss."' Source: *China Business Review*, Nov–Dec 2001

A Cap Gemini survey of 700 global companies reported that the length of an employee's tenure was primarily determined by the employee's relationship with their immediate manager.

Turnover is a global issue, felt keenly in developing and developed worlds alike. A study by the Hong Kong office of KPMG found that the average tenure for Chinese mid-to-senior-level executives in the People's Republic of China was 8–12 months. Since human resource expenditures generally run higher in foreign direct investment situations, the quality of human resources can often make or break whether a multinational's overseas venture succeeds. Keith Goodall and Willem Burgers of the China Europe International Business School noted in their article on the subject that poor retention of local staff ranks among the top three problems that foreign companies face.[38] This may be in part because the concept of career development is still relatively new in China and newer still for young Chinese.

Staff retention is an issue that Hong Kong and Shanghai Banking Corp. (HSBC) takes very much to heart. HSBC is an international financial services corporation with business arms in nearly 80 countries and a track record of low employee attrition. The cultivation of local managerial staff is extremely important to the bank's global market strategy, particularly in the emerging markets of the Pacific Rim. To demonstrate its commitment to local employees and the seriousness with which it takes the retention-issues surrounding talented young Asian professionals, HSBC instituted a novel program for its Chinese managers in the late 1990s.

The program gave newly appointed HSBC Chinese managers the opportunity to travel to Britain for a 10-week training program and to participate in additional follow-up training in both Britain and Hong Kong over a successive three-year period. High-performing trainees were then eligible for fast-track promotion as HSBC rotated out expatriate managers and replaced a given number with home-grown talent each year. As further inducement to build their careers with HSBC in China, the bank rounded out its package by granting recruits special bonuses for completing their coursework and providing discounted mortgage loans for those interested in purchasing a home.[39]

By presenting local market candidates with strong training, clear career development options, competitive compensation, and the chance to grow quickly into general management roles, HSBC—which calls itself "the world's local bank"—will likely sustain its reputation for low turnover and capitalize on the merits of a motivated and committed workforce.

EXTENDING THE NOTION OF VALUE-ADDED TO EMPLOYEE DEVELOPMENT

The 2005 edition of the *Financial Times* (*FT*) newspaper's annual "Best Workplaces" survey reveals five recurring themes among the happiest workplaces. They include: support at work; support at home; work/life balance; career development; and, trust. Together these qualities help employees feel valued and respected, resulting in a more committed and productive workforce.[40]

To support employees at home, the *FT* reported that several of the top scoring companies offer mentoring and coaching. Some, like P&G, even allow the employee to choose their own coach, someone whose experience and accomplishments match the employee's own aspirations. Mentors at WL Gore Associates are given active training to enable on-the-ground, effective coaching, rather than simply throwing the adviser in cold.

BMW—Lifetime Employment

"The lifetime employment system that BMW provides is a guarantee for people to have the freedom to express their opinions and their ideas, develop the business and themselves without fear for their own future. It is key to the strength of our corporate culture and one of the reasons for our low attrition rate." *Stefan Krause, CFO, BMW Group*

Time and again, the *FT* observed the impact corporate support of an employee's personal life had on the employee's perception of the company. When the individual suffered a death or illness in their family, top scoring companies showed sincere consideration. Unilever's Greek subsidiary provided a portable DVD player for an employee's hospitalized sister and paid for the employee to make several trips back to England to visit her. Beyond personal emergencies, employees in the most contented corporations also appreciated company efforts at smoothing work/life balance through flexible hours or work-at-home arrangements.

Not surprisingly, career development resonated strongly with most employees. Some of the best companies take strides to tailor personal development plans that expose the individual to challenging assignments in-house, as well as the opportunity to serve outside the company for a period. Katsuaki Watanabe, the president of Toyota Motor Company stresses the importance of doing this. He says, "Instead of isolating specialists from the rest of the group, I place people with different expertise into a large room and let them work together. They come from various divisions such as design, development, finance, procurement and human resources. They are forced to bring down the barriers that may divide them by functions and learn to collaborate as a team."[41]

Perhaps the most critical theme highlighted in the *FT's* report is the importance of trust. The happiest employees did not feel they had to punch their proverbial time card in at the start and end of each day. Instead, they were trusted to manage their jobs as professionals. If they needed to work from home, they could. If they had to leave early or arrive late, they could. As one P&G employee noted in the survey, "Each individual can decide what they need to do and how they need to run their life in order to deliver."[42]

It's clear that the corporate emphasis on "adding value" applies every bit as much to employee development and retention programs as it does to satisfying external customers.

UNLEASHING POWER TO RETAIN THE BEST

Consistent management and leadership attention to building meaningful relationships with star employees may be on most "to do" lists. The problem is that few executives have the bandwidth to perform this task given the extraordinary demands they face.

To address this, thoughtful leaders build supporting systems to foster necessary personal and professional development. Stanford's Professor Pfeffer explains that visionary leaders, "see their roles as systems architects, engaged in the critical task of building values, cultures, and a set of management practices that enable the recruitment, retention, development, and motivation of outstanding people."[43] This is done in recognition of the fact that while strategy is important, executing against that strategy is even more critical.

While businesses are not democracies, global competition may require that companies reassess their organizational structure. In a bid to attract the most talented employees and adapt quickly to changing global customer needs, companies may move away from "command and control" structures and shift instead to a distributed management approach. By disaggregating power, companies can vest employees with more meaningful responsibilities and potentially unleash faster decision-making and response times.

ORGANIZATIONAL DESIGN—BUILDING A HOME YOUR EMPLOYEES CAN LOVE

Conventional wisdom holds that a company's strategy should dictate the type of structure a business develops. If, for example, you determine that you are going to be a high-end luxury goods retailer, you do not place your stores in run-down sections of town. Suppliers, distributors, staffing and pricing are all dictated by the market strategy you employ. The premise is logical. The management team constructs a business model based on a chosen strategic plan and then configures the organization's structure in support of that plan.

If strategies change as, of course, they must in light of competition, then the company's organizational structure adjusts accordingly. Small companies are used to this process, accustomed by necessity to shuffling processes in response to near constant changes in customer demands and needs. Large companies are also used to driving and responding to change, but their bulk can make transforming underlying processes in support of new initiatives a much more complex and challenging prospect.

If enduring business success depends upon human resource talent and their ability to delight customers (whose needs and location are constantly growing), what organizational structure best allows ambitious global companies to challenge and retain the best and the brightest?

Consider the different organizational forms that exist. While there are many variations, the majority can be distilled into three main types:

❏ The Departmental Structure in which the organization is broken down by functional and business unit or product lines.
❏ The Matrix Structure in which the organization's managers represent a function, a product line a business unit or product, an operation and/or a region (the specific nature of which depends on the company).
❏ The Distributed Management or Network Structure in which the organization is comprised of several self sufficient operating units working together.

Departmental Structure

As manufacturing entities embraced the assembly line, employee groups were organized around discrete production activities, fitting a car engine onto a chassis, for example. A process manager would oversee one part of the completed project. A unit manager would oversee the engine manager's work and coordinate its place in the larger product manufacturing scheme. These unit managers reported up through the chain of command, uniting disparate divisional functions and activities.

In this fashion, the pyramid reporting structure stream-lined interchange. Departmentalizing by function gave companies the opportunity to combine specialized tasks into a functioning whole. From this starting point, many companies evolved specialized sub-divisions within larger departments in response to growing product complexity. A given function, such as marketing, might have several specialized marketing units housed within it. This efficient structure has been a critical aspect of corporate success throughout much of the twentieth century.

Such an environment is in wide use today. However, in his book, *The New Managerial Economics*, Professor William Boyes describes the development of various organizational forms. Boyes indicates that while the multi-divisional form of management works well, it can be vulnerable in a few important areas—namely, when shrinking product lives and customer sophistication call for greater cross-disciplinary engagement or when the costs of maintaining the departmentalized structure outweigh the benefits.[44]

Boyes notes that Pepsi found itself temporarily hamstrung by its formal departmental structure in the 1980s. The problem arose when supermarkets, one of Pepsi's largest customer groups, began converging into larger regional and pan-regional chains. Since Pepsi was structured geographically, some supermarket operating groups had to figure out which of several different Pepsi regional divisions it should call to do business, since its company now covered several Pepsi areas, a situation that uncorrected, could have led to much confusion.

Matrix Structure

In response, Pepsi turned to a matrix structure, one that Boyes noted appealed to many companies for its increased flexibility. A matrix structure allows a company's divisions and functions to organize along multiple dimensions. For example, a software company might build itself along vertical industry lines led by one group of executives. The company might also want specialization by business activity, so another axis of the matrix might focus on separate business functions, such as, general ledger, payroll, and tax preparation software, each headed by its own executive group.

To coordinate global activities, the software company might build out a geographical reporting line, featuring national, regional and global leaders as appropriate. Employees and managers would have multiple reporting lines. For instance, a given payroll product manager might report through the health-care industry chief and also to the regional director for Europe. In this way, the matrix structure allows diverse but important business strands to be woven together, paving the way for greater teaming and innovation. Customers benefit from this as well as from the streamlined point of contact.

Nothing is perfect, however. While the benefits of a matrix organizational structure are compelling, it may not work for all organizations. Layered reporting lines can facilitate interchange, but can occasionally become encumbered by bureaucracy. It can be costly to manage the increased complexity of the business. In addition, the larger and more complex the business organization, the larger and more complex the matrix required. Coordinating and managing the logistics surrounding that can act as a drag on executing changes in strategy.

Distributed Management

In light of this, some global businesses are turning to a more distributed form of management. This setting allows work groups to organize along a number of dimensions in a loose structure, each of which may operate on a quasi-autonomous basis, while reporting into global leadership. Some may rely on standardized shared services across the enterprise while carrying out the remainder of their tasks independently.

The global advertising and marketing services business, Omnicom, is a good example of the power of the network-driven organization. Although Omnicom is made up of many self-contained operating units, including several competing advertising agencies, they are all tightly connected to the core business.

Omnicom's network structure is carefully planned. To expand, they add more entities or clients. To contract, they divest. This gives the company flexibility in responding to changes in strategy, in the economic environment, and client needs. As the KPMG LLP (U.S.) book *Risk: From the CEO and Board Perspective* commented:

> "The portfolio of clients is such that none pose a disproportionate business risk . . . 'there's no one place, no one client that is significant enough to Omnicom that if there

were a breakdown it would put the company, or the things we worry about, in serious jeopardy."

The balanced "tension" is Omnicom's way of trying to stay ahead of the risk curve. Says CEO Wren, "No single discipline is large enough to dominate how resources are allocated. . . . [Secondly] no geography is overexposed by a preponderance of clients. And, third is the competitive nature of our businesses among themselves. We have multiple subsidiaries servicing the same client, but not under the same central leadership."[45]

The network structure can confer important advantages to a global competitor:

❏ *Self-sufficient and fast*—The self-sufficiency of the network structure can enable the company to robustly manage many activities simultaneously. Management can "plug on" or "detach" parts, allowing the company to more quickly respond to unpredictable market pressures across their global footprint. This distributed management form can assist companies operating in multiple foreign markets manage diversification and an ever-broadening scope of customer needs.

❏ *Suited to Capturing Competitive Intelligence*—As your company's "outer eyes and ears," employees in a disaggregated, local-market-facing environment play a key role in relaying important customer feedback through the corporate ecosystem.

❏ *Attractive and challenging work environment*—Under a network form of management, a company's individual business units are often smaller and focused on a particular product or service or one aspect of the customer experience. As small, semi-autonomous units, employees may be able to move more swiftly through tasks and positions, keeping them both challenged and stimulated, while providing valuable training.

Choosing the right "home" that your employees will love depends a lot on your business, your culture and your employees. Employees must be vested in the design since they are ultimately responsible for executing on the strategy that flows from it. Like most things truly thoughtful, there is no one "right" solution. The dynamics of the global marketplace, however, confer some advantage to a distributed network organization, one that fosters self-sufficiency, responsiveness, employee empowerment, and the competitor intelligence benefit of local "eyes and ears." Whatever form of organization a company ultimately takes, one law remains immutable. The company must maintain a delicate balance between global leadership and empowered local management. Global competitiveness demands it.

ENLIGHTENED SELF INTEREST

The role of the CEO is to balance an enterprise's important financial and operational goals against what former AT&T executive Chester Barnard, quoted in a Harvard Business School article, called, "the enduring purpose and values that is the foundation for meaningful action."[46]

A philosophical sea change is taking place in some corporate boardrooms. A desire to be "in balance" with our people, our environment and our business partners is fueling thoughtful discussion. It centers on this: the most enduring businesses will be those in which stakeholders take and are permitted a vested interest and then share in the results.

Corporate Social Responsibility

The rise of Corporate Social Responsibility (CSR) has been one response to stakeholder calls for business to become more active in improving environmental and social quality in the communities in which it operates. But here we must be careful.

Corporate Social Responsibility

"CSR is about reciprocal obligations." Professor Richard Welford, Professor of Corporate Environmental Governance, University of Hong Kong. *Source: South China Morning Post, April 2005*

There is a tendency to adopt new trends wholeheartedly—the all or nothing response. Thus Corporate Social Responsibility, as interpreted by some, can spawn a wide-ranging menu of philanthropic and good citizen programs. That a company has a moral responsibility to contribute to appropriate charitable causes, improve the quality of the environment (particularly if one is actively soiling it), and ensure one's own production and labor practices are clean, fair, equitable and safe, is not in dispute. As with all things, however, discretion and strategy must come into play.

Britain's political and current affairs newspaper, *The Economist*, for example, has taken public issue with the hook, line and sinker adoption of some corporate social responsibility practices. While they laud charitable giving, the newspaper argues that if the company is public, the funds being donated are not those of the CEO or executive management, but of the shareholders. They postulate that in contributing shareholder money to well-intentioned community efforts, management may unintentionally be diluting shareholder wealth.

> ### CSR as a Continuum
>
> John A. Quelch, Senior Associate Dean, International Development and Lincoln Filene Professor of Business Administration, Harvard Business School, described CSR as a continuum with philanthropy at one end, win-win skills leveraged in the middle, and deliberately making CSR part of the business model at the other end. *Source: WEF, 2005*

As practitioners, observers and critics alike may note, there are several types of corporate social responsibility. One is the purely philanthropic model just referred to, which is laudable in its aims, but potentially wasteful or misdirected in other respects. Another is a more calculating kind. A company may put on a veneer of corporate social responsibility to grease its reputation. For instance, a manufacturer may perform token environmental clean-ups, but not really commit to changing underlying processes. The disingenuousness aids no one, of course. In the long-term, even the company itself can become tainted by its own cultural effluent as employees react to the lack of sincerity. This is, after all, one of the fastest ways to sour employee trust in an organization.

This leaves a third, and we think, better form of Corporate Social Responsibility, one in which decisions are made based on what best supports the business, its employees and its network of corporate and community relationships. Pursued in this manner, CSR is good business, but with richer dimensions. Procter &Gamble (P&G) gave it a name in fact. They call it Corporate Social Opportunity.

In an interview with *The Development Gateway*, George Carpenter, Director of Corporate Sustainable Development at P&G, reflected on his organization's concern over the value of P&G's environmental group back in 1999. The company had made a tremendous investment in a number of environmental innovations in both their products and their packaging. However, Carpenter acknowledged, "We never really created a competitive advantage in the sense of a new business; we achieved savings from materials reduction and saved bottom line cost, but we never created new consumers, new markets and new products despite fairly sizable investments. As a result green marketing had a bad name in our marketing department, in our company and across the business in general."[47]

In response, P&G rethought its approach and introduced the business-community notion of sustainability. The result was a series of smart, market capturing moves that leveraged innovation, aided the community, and delivered practical benefits to P&G's bottom line.

This was triggered in part by P&G's observation at the uptick in digital communications in poorer parts of the world. Carpenter noted that while cell phones were a luxury item in many parts of North America and Europe, they were a common, everyday accessory for people in places like Mexico City where traditional phone service was sporadic. (Mexico was the first country in North America to operate a cellular phone system, in 1981.)

This led P&G to think differently about the developing world. Rather than assume that what works for the developed world works for everyone, P&G reflected on some of the unique needs of poorer markets. Resulting products included a line of children's juices loaded with nutrients that impoverished children might otherwise lack, as well as PUR, a water purification product that has the ability to turn 10 liters of dirty water clean in 15 minutes.[48]

By developing products such as these, P&G is making not only a moral contribution to some of the world's neediest peoples, but is also building the groundwork for what it is convinced will be the growing marketplace of the future. As Carpenter observed, "Our CEO has spoken of developing country markets as a huge source of income growth for P&G in the future."[49] In this respect, P&G strategically-directed Corporate Social Opportunity initiatives benefit its stakeholders and shareholders alike. And, that is good business.

CSR as a Competitive Tool

CSR can be an extraordinary means of building credibility with employees and customers. During the 2005 World Economic Forum in Davos, Switzerland, Orin Smith, Chief Executive Officer of Starbucks Coffee, described how his company deliberately weds CSR into the business model in part to be sensitive to the community and in part to hold on to valued employees. Since customer service, Smith said, is the cornerstone of Starbucks' success, the way they retain that advantage is by making sure that Starbucks is the kind of company people want to work for. While the company is a leader in ensuring that coffee bean producers make a livable wage, they are equally bold in making sure that their employees receive important benefits such as tuition reimbursement, personal career development and comprehensive health care, for both full-time and part-time employees (a rare offering in today's expensive health-care environment).

According to *Fortune Magazine*, the strategy is working. For the sixth year in a row, *Fortune* ranked Starbucks in their annual "Top 100 Companies to Work For" list.

NEW LEADERSHIP REQUIREMENTS

The simple vision espoused in this chapter is rooted in what we call the prosperity principle, where the organization's well-being is dependent not only on financial success, but also on a thriving and productive workforce. Prosperous companies are by their nature more competitive, with hearts and minds engaged toward a common goal. Organizations will have many ways of defining the necessary employee empowered culture. The following leadership requirements are indicative of some characteristics that are common among enduring, prosperous businesses.

People Principles

❏ Establish Work/Life Leadership
  ○ Create a "tone at the top" that encourages a positive work/life blend and a culture of shared ideals, recognizing that the CEO is the architect of organizational values.
  ○ Healthy work/life relationships spur improved productivity. Encourage management and employees to invest time in building strong professional relationships in the workplace and reward substantive employee/management connections with the community.
  ○ Bureaucracy stymies motivation. Direct leadership to minimize review streams and "red tape" to improve responsiveness and execution. Encourage senior leadership to intervene more directly, personally and frequently with business units.
❏ Foster a Development Culture to Unleash Talent
  ○ Tailor a professional development plan for core employees that goes beyond the annual goal setting process. Cultivate active, committed and long-term mentoring relationships. Help mentors become comfortable and effective by providing appropriate training. And, pair employees with mentors who match the employee's career achievement goals.

○ Promote high performers early in order to continually raise the performance bar and keep key talent
stimulated.

○ Cultivate local staff to support, and eventually re-
place, expatriate management, as appropriate. As
owners of local relationships, the value of highly-
qualified local and regional management will increase significantly. Effectively educating, empowering and motivating these individuals will become
paramount.

❑ Build a Workplace Employees will Love

○ Accept some natural democratization of process,
power and profits as this will allow for the most efficient execution of their business plans and foment
the most spirited innovation.

○ While one's industry, objectives and culture dictate
the optimal organizational structure, the dynamics
of the global marketplace confer some advantage to
a distributed network organization, one that fosters
self-sufficiency, responsiveness, employee empowerment, and the competitor intelligence benefit of local
eyes and ears.

○ Employees want to feel good about the place they
work. Corporate Social Responsibility initiatives em-
body the company's character and values and
demonstrate them in action. Used strategically
rather than purely philanthropically, CSR can be an
extraordinary means of building credibility with employees, customers and shareholders.

CONCLUSION

Renowned management author and Harvard Business School Professor Rosabeth Moss Kanter, appearing at a World Economic Forum panel that imagined what companies would be like in the year 2020 said, "The 2020 company's values will be courage, compassion, competency and integrity."[50] In that environment, she pointed out, "The institution becomes more important than the person even when the person's name is on the door . . ." and demonstrates "that you are building something greater than yourselves, something that survives after you, and adds value to the world." In this new and burgeoning information age, a company's human assets are its most valuable. The most competitive business organizations will find a way to channel both the intellectual and spiritual energy of its workforce. Those entities will build a culture of shared ideals in which personal and business goals will become increasingly intertwined in pursuit of a progressive and prosperous partnership for the future.

CHAPTER 4

Building Value Through Effective Global Operations

"If you don't have a global perspective and you're not playing a global game, you are vulnerable."

—John Pizzey, CEO of Australian automotive manufacturer ION

In a given day around the world, FedEx answers 500,000 telephone calls, receives 63 million electronic transmissions, flies 638 aircraft, lands at 365 airports, drives 43,000 vehicles some 2.7 million miles (in the U.S.), stops at 34,000 drop boxes, and manages 3.1 million packages.

Operations Management

Pertains to the series of activities that relate to the company's production of a good or service. It includes procurement, inventory control, quality control, storage, logistics and evaluations.

The first company to offer overnight delivery back in the early 1970s, FedEx has retained its leadership status by investing in a sophisticated operational core that has earned it the lion's share of the express delivery business worldwide. So dependable, responsive and fast is FedEx, that *Business-Week* once reported that Merrill Lynch & Co employees used the service to deliver documents between floors of its Manhattan headquarters. Employees felt FedEx was just that much faster and more reliable than Merrill's own interoffice deliveries.

As companies gird themselves to compete with the vigor demanded by our burgeoning global economy, some, like FedEx, are using operations excellence to differentiate their value proposition. In fact, FedEx's innovations proved so groundbreaking that it has since spun its expertise into separate supply chain and logistics businesses that today serve corporate customers around the world.

As leaders assess the best way to grow their businesses for the long-term, this chapter offers an important perspective on optimizing the business from the inside-out, through effective global operations.

DRIVING VALUE FROM OPERATIONS

Operations used to be thought of as a commodity, a necessary function that supported company strategy but did not necessarily inform it. That is changing.

Consider these dynamics. Manufacturing is leading the global flight from the developed world to the developing. Multinational companies are turning to outsourcing in increasing numbers to take advantage of the low-wage arbitrage offered by nations such as Mexico, China and India. Added to this, supply chains are getting longer as companies apply a sharper focus to those activities they do best and rely on partners to support the rest.

Underlying these activities is a tremendous reliance on the operational core of an organization. Issues such as cost management, financial restructuring, plant and distribution location, inventory and capacity all weigh into the calculus that guides corporate strategy. Operations executives must determine how to steer their function forward in a way that advances business strategy while responding to ever changing variables in consumer taste and the marketplace in general.

For guidance in responding to these daunting demands, we look at how some of the best, Dell, Toyota Motor Company and later IBM, are reengineering their operations to enable more swift, efficient, and responsive output, at lower cost.

Lean and Mean: Dell Delivers

The easy-money days of the 1990s proved an attractive time for many companies to pursue wide-ranging business-to-business, business-to-consumer, supply chain, customer relationship management, and other initiatives. With so much activity to chase, traditional aspects of operations management often received short shrift. Only when the global economy applied its brakes at the end of the century did some companies retrain their focus to trim waste, tighten process flow and maximize efficiency.

Dell Computer had already cultivated a habit of challenging conventional wisdom. Unlike some competitors, the "operations as revenue generator" angle was one they understood early. After all, the company had turned the traditional computing business model on its head in the late 1990s when it eliminated the reseller and began retailing directly to consumers, an almost heretical concept at the time.

By doing away with the reseller and tightly automating its production and sales activities, Dell was able to control the entire revenue stream. Consumers shopped for, designed and purchased their computer all online, with the new model arriving at their doorstep a few days later. The savings Dell generated from its stripped down processes were passed on to consumers, improving margins and market share in the same stroke. In these and other ways, operations defined Dell's corporate and competitive strategy.

Given its history, you would expect that a company whose external edge was so driven by technology would be similarly wired internally. Not so, or at least not so to the same degree. Indeed, one can imagine Michael Dell's chagrin back in 1999 when he looked at his procurement and conversion processes and observed that the bulk of them were, in fact, being driven manually.

Reporting on what it called Dell's "second web revolution," *BusinessWeek* noted that Dell's operational overhaul began in 1999 with an e-mail from Michael Dell to his supply-chain group. In it he enquired why the company that was the hands-down leader in e-commerce sales wasn't "eating their own dog food" and using its technology to speed and refine its procurement processes.[51] That conclusion led him to push his operations team to transform.

> ### The Dell Advantage
>
> "Eleven years ago, Dell carried 20–25 days of inventory in a sprawling network of warehouses. Today, it has no warehouses. And, although it assembles nearly 80,000 computers every 24 hours, it carries no more than two hours of inventory in its factories and a maximum of 72 hours across its entire operation." *Source: Fast Company, Issue 88*

They got the message. Today, Dell's core suppliers are required to have a physical plant near Dell's manufacturing facility in Austin, Texas. Not only are the suppliers physically connected to the pulse of Dell's operation, but they are also electronically embedded into one of the most sophisticated procurement webs in the business. When an assembly line runs low on disk drives or other parts, it sends a signal to its supplier.

As *Fast Company* magazine observed, that supplier then has 90 minutes to deliver the parts to Dell's plant. It can't be early and it can't be late. When the tractor trailer arrives (at one of 110 cargo bays circling Dell's plant) it waits. At the moment the new disk drives are needed, a forklift removes the desired quantity from the trailer onto the factory floor. In characteristic Dell style, the disk drives are recorded as purchased only after the forklift crosses a built in bar code scanner that is embedded into the factory floor a few feet in from the cargo bay.[52]

As one might gather, for Dell, inventory is a ball and chain, a weighty drag to be avoided at all costs. While some computer manufacturers rely on an inventory cushion of 3–6 weeks, Dell keeps only the supplies it needs to keep production running for two hours at the most.

Such lean and mean manufacturing tactics confer a strategic advantage in a margin tight industry like computing. Roger Kay, of the research house IDC, observed that, "Various industry assessments report that Dell's cost advantage through close-to-zero inventory is as high as eight points, which in a commodity business is huge."[53] This gives Dell huge maneuvering room to outmuscle peers.

The Dell story illustrates not only one company's innovation, but also the highly significant role operations play in catapulting a company into a dominant market position.

For operational excellence on a truly global scale, we turned to Caterpillar, the world's leading manufacturer of construction and mining equipment, diesel and natural gas engines and industrial gas turbines. Much of the company's operational backbone is tied to its commitment to 6 Sigma, Caterpillar's framework for improving performance. CEO, Jim Owens, stated, "We have a fully integrated manufacturing presence in every continent and major currency zone, and we have dealers that more than double our capital and number of employees. This combines to give us an exceptionally strong local presence everywhere we do business." [54]

Owens adds, "What distinguishes us from our competition is that we have a really holistic business model, meaning that we not only design and manufacture engines, but we sell them as well. We have a strong distribution network. We have a services business. We're in the used equipment business. We finance the product. We insure the product and we're involved in customer support like no one else. So, we really have the full life cycle of the machine covered. And that makes it hard for somebody to sneak up on us."

Indeed, Caterpillar's 6 Sigma methodology has become a pervasive instrument in squeezing optimum performance from the company's various operating units. The company credits 6 Sigma with enabling its dramatic improvement in 2004 profitability, with machinery and engine sales increasing by an unprecedented 35% in 2004. "The advantage of 6 Sigma in a big company like ours," says David Burritt, VP and current CFO, "is that it provides a strategic selection filter." Any large company, he asserts, is buffeted by many different projects and many competing priorities. 6 Sigma allows you to isolate those things that are truly most important.

So committed is Caterpillar to the benefits of the program, that it is actively engaged in driving the discipline into 380 of Caterpillar's key suppliers. "Before," Burritt observed, "every unit, every customer, every dealer solved problems on their own. Now, we have a globally consistent methodology with which to continuously improve quality." It's not that

6 Sigma offers radically new thinking, he stresses. It's that it confers a rigor and a discipline that allows Caterpillar to trace financial benefits directly to the bottom line.

Speed and Responsiveness:
The Toyota Production System

The quality of one's operations and internal processes is inextricably linked to speed and responsiveness. While there is no "one-size-fits-all" approach to world leading operations, companies at the forefront of global competition are redesigning production processes to integrate and streamline routine activities. In addition, they are rethinking customer facing activities to provide superior customization, innovation and responsiveness.

Just-in-Time

Kiichiro Toyoda, founder of the Toyota automobile business, developed the concept of Just-in-Time in the 1930s. He ruled that Toyota operations would contain no excess inventory and that Toyota would work in partnership with suppliers to level production.

Process redesign is something that Toyota Motor Corporation knows quite a lot about. Says Katsuaki Watanabe, president of Toyota, "It takes close teamwork and partnership inside and outside the company to make a perfect car."[55] As a consequence, over the years, the famed Toyota Production System has churned out more than just good cars. They have also produced management principles of world renown.

Concepts such as Just-in-Time and Lean Production were both invented inside the company walls.

Developed by Toyota Chief of Production, Taiichi Ohno in the 1950s, the Toyota Production System (TPS) has since become the subject of many research papers and books. The ground-breaking MIT work *The Machine that Changed the World* brought worldwide attention to Toyota's production processes and christened the term *lean production*.

> ### Toyota Production System
>
> "The Toyota Production System is at the heart of everything we do. Based on the concept of continuous improvement, or kaizen, every Toyota team member is empowered with the ability to improve their work environment. This includes everything from quality and safety to the environment and productivity. Improvements and suggestions by team members are the cornerstone of Toyota's success."
> *Source: Toyota Motor Corporation Website*

In designing TPS, Ohno leveraged the *jidoka* (automation with human intelligence) quality improvement practices created by Sakichi Toyoda, father of Toyota Motor's founder Kiichiro Toyoda, and integrated it with process improvement tools such as Just-in-Time, Total Quality Control, Kaizen, small-lot production and others. The initial focus was on redesigning the inner workings of the machine shop. But today, Ohno's streamlined, highly-efficient processes penetrate all aspects of Toyota production; touching every machine, every production line and every Toyota operation.

Activity is driven by webs of teams interacting together. If one link fails, the system goes down. The bottom-up process means that TPS is led by the associates working the shop floor. Toyota's management serve as mentors rather than overseers, offering guidance and ensuring that teams have the necessary tools, resources and supplies to get their jobs done.

The value of TPS relies upon more than the Just-in-Time, Total Quality Control and the other aforementioned principles. It stems from the symbiosis of its supporting systems. Each step informs and relies upon others in the chain.[56] Watanabe adds, "The key to success is finding a perfect combination of the best global and the best local technology. The rigid organization cannot allow flexible combinations between various types of technology. You have to be flexible enough to encourage optimal forms of collaboration."

Toyota's "2010 Global Vision"guides the company's long-term innovation. The company is using its strong balance sheet, gained in part from TPS and industry leading efficiency levels, to expand production facilities overseas and invest in trend-setting new car models, such as its popular hybrids. With five years to go, success is showing. Toyota is now second only to General Motors, and *Fortune* magazine has ranked Toyota the fifth most admired company in the world on its 2005 "Global All-Stars List."

FINANCIAL EDGE

As we have seen, innovations in how a company sources, manufactures and distributes its product can combine to increase sales and market share. The best ensure output that is streamlined and swift. This provides an important financial edge in terms of revenue generation, as discussed, as well as cost management. In too many organizations, however, the latter is done reflexively.

When a downturn strikes, knee-jerk cuts can ensue. Generally, among the most immediate targets are discretionary spending items such as travel, advertising, training and product development. Also common is an across-the-board personnel or budget cut of a given percentage. These practices, while prompted by necessary competitive realities, often fail to deliver the "lean and mean" results desired. That is to say, they may make the company leaner, but, if done *reflexively* and not *reflectively*, can also make the company weaker. By aligning cost improvement opportunities with individual business requirements, one advances both superior process efficiency as well as cost improvements.

Restructuring Global Operations: IBM

In May 2005, IBM announced a massive and deep restructuring of its global operations. It would reduce the size of its European headquarters, minimize its presence in Europe and increase its presence in other parts of the globe.[57]

While the moves have a clear short-term objective, namely, to lower IBM's costs and improve its margins, IBM had a rough first quarter in 2005. The restructuring has been planned for a while. With the increasing sophistication of emerging competitors from around the world putting pressure on its current business model, IBM is seeking to transform the way it competes. The company's CFO, Mark Loughridge, underscored this, stating, "We are moving toward more globally-integrated operations, while improving efficiency as we continue to focus on the systems and services technology for enterprise and business clients."[58]

In an effort to become both faster and more responsive, IBM is flattening its hierarchy and distributing its management power, putting more authority in the hands of in-country and regional centers of excellence. The centers will localize responsibility for procurement and service delivery and seek to sharply improve efficiency. As IBM Vice President Bob Moffat observed in *BusinessWeek*, "We're lowering our center of gravity and globalizing our delivery."[59] All cuts are painful. But the fact that IBM's operational transition is wedded to its unfolding global strategy augurs well for its success.

Like IBM's effort, strategic cost assessments should be an ongoing activity regardless of whether times are good or difficult. To help them along, cost reductions should be governed by tight controls and regularly evaluated to assess their performance impact. Any refinements must support the underlying operational processes. These should be periodically adjusted against changes in corporate strategy.

LEVERAGING COMPLIANCE TO ACHIEVE LASTING VALUE[60]

As we have seen, a company can secure a substantial competitive lead before the product or service leaves its doors. In doing so, it searches for opportunities to remove redundancies, improve controls, and eradicate execution bottlenecks at every turn.

Such a process might entail costly investment. Perhaps unexpectedly, the regulatory process offers some relief. That is because in the case of most publicly held U.S. companies, Sarbanes-Oxley section 404 (S-O 404) compliance efforts give them a head start, even if indirectly. A significant chunk of time, dollar and resource investment has already been made. Proactive companies are using the results of that compliance exercise to their advantage.

> *Operations Return on Investment (ROI)*
>
> "Sarbanes-Oxley is a steep new cost, with direct accountability by the CEO and all executives, but with the total cost of control and return on investment squarely in the hands of the operations executive."
> *Source: "The Operations Track" by Greg Smith, Steve Hill, John Rittenhouse, KPMG LLP (U.S.) in Forum magazine.*

AMR Research estimates that companies collectively will spend $5.8 billion in 2005 to meet S-O requirements.[61] From their compliance efforts, companies have now amassed large volumes of documented controls data.[62] As a consequence, managers today have at their disposal valuable insight into what types of controls are in place, what they are monitoring and who is responsible for them. Precisely because Sarbanes-Oxley requires such heightened introspection, it can be the catalyst for a new level of operational controls, visibility and value.

This is because operations, by their nature, drive financial value. S-O 404 documentation provides operations leaders with the opportunity to scrutinize the interrelatedness of their operational controls. Used as a blueprint to identify current state, gaps and future benchmarks, the operations function can utilize its internal controls information to identify opportunities to improve efficiency while reducing compliance risk, leading, in turn, to more informed decision-making.

We highlight some of the major advantages here:

Standard View

For example, an operations manager can use the S-O 404 process to drive consistent standards across their enterprise. In doing so, he or she can eliminate overlapping controls and institute more reliable quality levels.

Take, for instance, a major building materials company. That organization used the results of their S-O 404 compliance effort to facilitate a major process-improvement project. They assigned a dedicated project team to leverage their internal controls data and reverse engineer the company's income statement, balance sheet and disclosures. Any business process that fed into the financials was assigned a permanent team leader to design a set of standard internal controls best practices. Once collected, vetted and approved, the project team took the best practices around the world, traveling to over 100 worldwide locations to communicate and train colleagues. As a result, the building materials company now has a standard set of internal-controls best practices in place throughout the company everywhere it operates.[63]

Accuracy and Reliability

Without effective controls over its procurement processes, companies can experience unwanted balance sheet volatility and uneven inventory capacity. These disconnects can be avoided when financial controls are better connected to the company's business performance controls.

Most retail companies, for example, have multiple buyers servicing a variety of categories in the company's portfolio. They may make individual buying decisions based on their estimate of expected future volume, a practice that may be removed from an analysis of the company's current purchasing commitments or spending capability. In matters such as these, S-O 404 documentation can provide better visibility across the board, supporting soft data with hard facts in order to identify financial and business control issues, improve these controls and create appropriate linkage.

Productivity

The tremendous automation that has resulted from the S-O 404 effort has transformed many formerly manual controls. Automated controls cannot only now detect problems, but in some cases prevent them from occurring at all. This allows more operations groups to function with improved predictability, alleviating production stoppages caused from line dysfunction or breakdowns, and improving ROI.

Because of the sheer volume of controls—in large organizations this numbers in the tens of thousands—the operations executive will be as intimately involved in Sarbanes-Oxley compliance as the chief financial officer. This gives them an unprecedented opportunity to use S-O 404 to improve business processes, operating margins and risk mitigation.

KNOWLEDGE MANAGEMENT

The "beyond compliance" activities of some companies prove once again that knowledge is power. Yet, real-time knowledge sharing remains elusive for many organizations. As intellectual capital accounts for an ever growing share of company asset value, those who can share and transfer knowledge most effectively will be at a distinct advantage.

The Internet ushered in the promise of tremendous knowledge management breakthroughs, but as many business people know only too well today, opening one's e-mail box in the morning and seeing several hundred unopened messages can fill one with a mixed sense of foreboding and tedium. Clearly, not all information is equally valuable. The wheat must be distilled from the chaff. This requires an organizational ability to filter and direct information that is correlated with the goals of the business and an equal ability to filter and direct non-essential information.

The process of collecting, sharing and storing useful knowledge is inherently mutable, with the knowledge itself quickly obsolete. In order to be meaningful and appeal to the

Getting Knowledge Management off the Ground

For knowledge management to take root, it must satisfy the following criteria:

❑ It must be practical, i.e., directly relate to one's work.

❑ It must be exhibit true thought leadership with respect to the company's strategy and mission.

❑ It must be meaningful, i.e., inspire or motivate employees to pull together to reach the organization's shared goals.

❑ It must be holistic, i.e., represent the full reach of the company's activities.

motivation levels of the knowledge workers who create and share it, namely ones' employees, knowledge management must create value.

Taking a Bite out of Knowledge Management: Frito-Lay

Frito-Lay, a US$9 billion subsidiary of Pepsi-Co, faced a problem experienced by many large companies. In an interview with *CIO* magazine in 2001, VP of Customer Development Mike Marino, stated, "We had knowledge trapped in files everywhere."[64] He knew that if only his team could find a way to access, share and communicate the same information consistently, it would alleviate a lot of problems. For example, he observed that many salespeople would turn to the company's marketing and operations staff and look for similar data and information. As a result, Frito-Lay's support staff were answering the same questions and performing the same functions over and over again. This was both time wasting and frustrating.

In addition, Marino knew that other information wasn't being captured at all, or if it was, it was being done inconsistently. Each sales person might have one part of the total information picture resident on his or her desktop, but rarely was a full customer view pieced together.

In response, Frito-Lay ran a pilot program in which it built an internal knowledge management portal—the first in Pepsi-Co, and one which would provide a single point of access to pertinent information in a secure, password-protected environment. The portal's goals were to "streamline data, exploit customer specific data and foster team collaboration."[65]

The sales team loaded the portal with customer and market data, sales and product information, news and analysis, and information on the company's "go-to" experts on different issues.

The results? While Marino expected his pilot team to outperform other sales groups without access to the Portal, even he was surprised at the extent of the group's success. While no specific figures were divulged, Marino said the "test team doubled the growth rate of the customer's business in the salty snack category." He added, "The retailer is happy because they're doing more business in their market and we're doing business at a faster growth rate with this customer than with other customers."[66]

Since knowledge management depends upon the efforts of its knowledge workers, members must be motivated to participate. As in the Frito-Lay case, participants must feel it is relevant to their work and to the profit-making activities of their organization. That is why a responsive global organization will view the knowledge-sharing function as intricately housed within its business and functional units.

Business unit leaders are already looked to as experts for a given function or industry group within their respective organizational cultures. It is as natural for an employee or manager to turn to that group with a specific client or process question as it would be for knowledge sharing. Like as not, the finding, creating, organization and communication of pertinent information are activities in which the unit is already fully engaged. The motivation for the business unit to take direct or indirect ownership of knowledge management is intrinsic.

For this reason we do not advocate isolating the knowledge function into a discrete group. In an effort to improve their knowledge management activities, a rush of Chief Knowledge Officers and related executives were hired by many companies. This trend is now dissipating. The fact is that successful knowledge management programs work more effectively and naturally within the business units and not juxtaposed alongside them, for the very reasons just elucidated.

CONCLUSION: MANAGING OPERATIONAL RISK

Companies pursue a menu of business modeling considerations as they plan their global enterprise. They can pursue scale not only across their organization, but also in given process areas as well. They can examine multiple sourcing options for given materials and a variety of plant or office locations in a way that balances economic, market, policy or other potential financial impacts. As they exploit factor cost differences, these same organizations will also consider ways to diversify their operational assets and ensure the right level of failure contingencies are in place.

Operational Visibility

Through their "controls lens," operations executives can answer several key questions:

- ❏ How do operational variations impact the balance sheet and income statement?

- ❏ How accurately is operations able to forecast supply and demand and product availability?

- ❏ How do business processes affect the company's return on investment?

Source: "Sarbanes-Oxley Compliance: The Compliance Track," KPMG LLP (U.S.), Forum magazine, Volume 6, Number 6/Q4.

Strategic Risk

Underlying these considerations is a recognition that global expansion makes sense for those industries that can best leverage it. For example, intellectual property and research and development entities tend to make good candidates. Consider a typical software company, where production costs move inverse to volume created. The incremental cost of each CD burned is marginal. It is harder, for example, for a distributor of a perishable commodity like tropical fruit, to enjoy the same economies as a silicon chip manufacturer. Factors such as transportation and distribution need to be considered as well.

Process Risk

Companies will be rewarded by taking the time to identify structural and process changes that enable sustainable, long-term efficiencies, even if the immediate payback is delayed. The driver should clearly be risk-based prioritization wherein management addresses those activities that stand to deliver the highest impact and potential for profitability first, while cultivating longer-term opportunities. Diversify operational risk to avoid the spectrum of labor wars, environmental, natural or political instability.

Control Risk

In our view, any operational risk category with enterprise-wide consequences should have an executive sponsor. As shareholders concentrate more and more on the risk-adjusted returns on their investment, company officers will be looking to balance their risk management and risk control activities with business and operational performance metrics. Leveraging the S-O effort and getting the right risk controls in place is one step. Linking them to the finance and operating functions is another.[67]

Performance Measurement

Performance measurement is critically important not only to gauge the quality of one's operations but also to manage risk. As a rule, the more attuned an organization is to indicators of unwanted volatility, the faster it is in preempting any negative consequences. Some companies deliberately "break" their systems as a means of periodically testing and refining critical performance areas. By analyzing their own processes in this way in a regular yearly check-up, they can better flag any serious weaknesses before a competitor can exploit it.

Conclusion

Going forward, strong operations management can provide companies with the ability to increase much needed operational visibility, boost overall business performance, and in the end, help make possible the financial transparency that stakeholders today demand.

CHAPTER 5

The Corporate Ecosystem

"The evolution of outsourcing points towards a new type of economic organization—a hybrid between a company and a market. . ."

—Ravi Aron, Assistant Professor, Wharton School, University of Pennsylvania, speaking at the 2005 World Economic Forum in Davos, Switzerland

For 10 days in October of 2002, cargo ships laden with Christmas presents lay grounded off the California coast. Fresh produce rotted as trucks idled in the Southern California heat. The labor dispute that pitted dockworkers against management at America's highest volume ports meant that some manufacturing operations across the United States slowed to a grind as needed parts remained holed up inside a flotilla of anchored ships.

The threat of a lockout had sent tremors throughout the U.S. and world economy. In Asia, stockpiles of cargo grew higher, lining the docks and causing local businesses to wonder if they would have to halt production. So tightly woven were international supply chains that manufacturers, distributors, retailers and consumers the world over worried about the ripple effect. Stephen Cohen, co-director of the Berkeley Roundtable on the International Economy, told the *L.A. Times* that, "If such a thing reaches a certain scale where the pain is really severe, you have an Asian financial crisis and an economic mess."[68]

As the specter of an impending port lockout grew, economists feared the cost to the U.S. economy could be as high as US$1 billion a day. Approximately 60% (or US$300 billion) of the cargo that comes into and goes out of the United States annually passes through West Coast ports, with items ranging from consumer goods and automobiles, to electronics and produce. The Pacific Maritime Association, a consortium that includes shipping lines and operators, predicted that the financial toll could reach US$19.4 billion.

In the end, however, despite the inevitable upheaval, the business community proved deft and responsive. Tallying up the damage, analysts and executives were, by and large, relieved to find that the actual costs from the labor stoppage were far lower than expected. While an exact figure is impossible to gauge, evidence suggests that the modern supply chain proved surprisingly robust.

It was that factor, the quality of the supply chain, that played a major role in how well companies fared. Scale, too, had a part. There is no question, for instance, that some small companies, like mom and pop retailers, and industries, like trucking, felt the impact keenly. Corporations with well-designed supply chains, however, proved far more resilient to the turbulence than peers with less dynamic systems.

Dell Computer, for one, was determined to be proactive in the face of the shutdown, deploying on-the-ground staff to move product in and around the Long Beach docks. Advance teams provided real-time information back to headquarters and took direct responsibility for loading and unloading certain cargo shipments.

With the waterways jammed, Dell took to the air, and was among the first to charter private aircraft to collect critical components from their manufacturers overseas. This solution kept Dell's finely tuned production running smoothly and ensured that their just-in-time assembly was not disrupted. By acting early, Dell managed to secure the most favorable chartering rates. Within short order, companies who were slower to respond to the unfolding situation found themselves scrapping over a limited supply of aircraft at prices double and triple normal rates.

Other companies showed similar dexterity. Produce giant Dole Food Company succeeded in re-routing its U.S. bound shipments of fruits and vegetables through Mexico and Alaska. This limited the company's losses dramatically during the period. In fact, Dole had originally estimated that the shutdown would cost their business nearly US$2.5 million. But because they were able to realign their supply structure, the final damage assessment came in sharply lower, between US$250,000 and US$500,000.[69]

The Long Beach dockworker dispute is illustrative on two fronts. First, it underscores how interconnected company supply chains have become and second the advantage a well managed chain can confer. This chapter will explore both points, as well as offer guidance to help business leaders in designing a competitive global supply chain.

THE MODERN GLOBAL SUPPLY CHAIN

The global supply chain holds the corporate ecosystem together, enabling the dynamic flow of goods, services, and other assets through and among a shifting set of business partners. Far from a simple structure, the activities embodied in today's supply chain encompass a diverse range of tasks, including sourcing and integration, portfolio optimization, demand and production planning, vendor rationalization, network planning and channel effectiveness. The way in which these flows are facilitated also varies widely, whether directly from department to department and partner to partner, or indirectly, via electronic exchanges that act as on-line supply chain marketplaces.

This marks a shift in understanding. Supply chains have traditionally been viewed as a set of linear connections, beginning with the sourcing of raw materials and concluding with the distribution of finished goods into the hands of the consumer. The reality, however, is that the modern supply chain is more concurrent than sequential, representing both the flow of goods and services *to* the customer, as well as, critically, the flow of issues and needs *from* the customer back through the supply chain. The throughput of product realization and customer reaction is interdependent. A sophisticated supply chain synchronizes its knowledge network to its production network and extends the links to non-traditional areas such as product innovation and the sales force. In this way, a good global supply chain not only supports a business but, done well, defines it. As Matsushita president, Kunio Nakamura, affirms, "We need to create an optimal supply chain structure which enables us to readily reflect the customer needs into our manufacturing process."[70]

Most major producers rely on a string of business partners to facilitate the movement of products into the hands of its consumers. An automobile manufacturer like General Motors, for example, might turn to the electronic exchange, Delphi, for needed parts, Union Pacific for logistics and AutoNation for retail support. A consumer goods manufacturer like Procter & Gamble might rely on DuPont for industrial supplies, Wakefern for distribution, Exel for global transportation and Albertsons supermarkets to place the product in the hands of the consumer. Similarly, the electronic components manufacturer Solestra might look to Quantum for storage devices, Ingram for channel support, FedEx for logistics, and Best Buy for retail.

The nature of the supply chain depends on the characteristics of the company, its industry, and moreover, its strategic business objectives. In all cases, the end game should be directed toward improving operating efficiencies and financial performance and, in the best cases, transforming and enhancing one's customer value proposition.

The prestige German car manufacturer, BMW Group, for instance, makes it a policy to seek long-term cooperation with its partners. Says group CFO, Stefan Krause, "We focus on networks in order to become faster and more flexible."[71] Adhering to the principle that he who works alone adds to his success, but he who works with others multiplies it, BMW Group relies on its global network of innovative partners, such as suppliers, high-tech businesses and research laboratories, to leverage and integrate needed production resources and collective innovation. Krause asserts, "Our networks are an external "breathing apparatus" and, at the same time, an appropriate way of catering for the future."

The benefits of an optimized supply chain are compelling, leading to a surge of interest in the topic and its adjuncts, offshoring and sourcing. Indeed, many industries have seen important bottom line benefits from improved supply chain processes. The automotive, oil and chemical and consumer goods sectors, in particular, have been effective at cultivating the commercial impact of their supply chain functions. With the carrying cost of inventory, the cost of storing and holding inventory, for many of these sectors ranging around 25% of product value, the *Economist* rightly observes that the costs of not managing the supply chain appropriately can be even higher.[72]

These developments have cast new light on what was once viewed as a rather humdrum activity. Before its strategic impact became well understood, the supply chain garnered relatively little attention. It was viewed commonly as a technology issue, something that the right software could fix. Today, a well-managed supply chain confers distinct advantages:

Growth & Development

- [ ] New delivery and distribution models
- [ ] Revenue enhancement and revenue assurance
- [ ] Improved customer satisfaction

Cost Management and Efficiency

- [ ] Reduced expenditures across the supply chain
- [ ] Tax efficiency
- [ ] Improved cycle times and reduced cash leakage
- [ ] End-to-end process automation

Managing Control and Compliance

- [ ] Enhance visibility of key metrics
- [ ] Provide tighter collaboration between trading partners
- [ ] Improve risk mitigation and reduce vulnerabilities throughout the chain

Even modest improvements in supply chain functionality can positively affect the quality of the income statement and balance sheet. Cycle time reductions, for instance, can boost revenue, lower expenses and engender healthier financial returns. Consider the quantitative leaps companies in Table 1 (see next page) achieved by improving the quality of their supply chain processes. By treating the supply chain strategically, companies acquire a means of achieving both short-term cost reductions and long-term business transformation.

Table 1: Bottom-line Impact—Representative List of Supply Chain Improvements

Benefit Area	Typical Improvements
Throughput	Up to 300% improvement
ROI	Up to 200% return
Inventory reduction	Up to 75% improvement
Cycle time	Up to 60% reduction
Delivery performance	Up to 50% improvement
Asset utilization	Up to 50% improvement
Productivity	Up to 30% improvement

Source: © 2005 KPMG International

Under the leadership of Toyota Motor President, Katsuaki Watanabe, Toyota introduced its Construction of Cost Competitiveness for the 21st Century (CCC21) program which sought to lower the cost of Toyota's parts and components by 30%. The company reexamined virtually every part that went into their automobiles. Not even the car's horn was spared. Six of the horn's 28 parts were eliminated along with 40% of associated cost.[73] So far, CCC21 has saved Toyota US$10 billion in the five years since Watanabe introduced the program. Toyota's relationship with its supply chain partners has been key to its success. Says Watanabe, "We maintain a culture where everyone participates in delivering quality improvements and cost reduction. This includes our suppliers." He adds, "We call them 'partners' because they are involved from the early stages of design all the way to the delivery of assembled cars. As a consequence, they are fully motivated to help us reduce the cost at every stage."[74]

COMPLEXITY

The challenge increasingly is delivering on these benefits. When companies do attempt to transform their supply chain, they often do so on a country or regional basis. That is because it is often quite difficult to stand back and look at an end-to-end supply chain on a global basis. The pressure to drive costs down, expand into new markets and innovate ever more quickly is causing system complexity to spiral.

Imagine a company that is rapidly trying to design, source, manufacture, sell and deliver a new product for a new market. Your chief suppliers are in China, India, and Eastern Europe. Your factories are in Brazil, China, and Taiwan, and your customers are in the United States, Europe and Japan. You are expected to launch in six months and believe your competitors are attempting to develop a rival product. Working capital is tight. As such, management has made it clear that you are to deliver on time and on budget. Margins must be preserved.

Far from an isolated "what if," this scenario is being played out in organizations around the world. Today's supply chains are under enormous pressure to deliver, which in turn propels high levels of complexity. Driving it are changes in financial and legal regulations, commercial market requirements, operating processes, information technology infrastructure, procurement, the absence of product standards in certain industries, and the nature and location of one's customer base.

Many executives agree that complexity is the chief bottleneck to supply chain optimization. Those companies that succeed in breaking through the morass are aggressively seeking to simplify their business. The best are rationalizing their core offerings, streamlining costs, focusing on primary brands and categories, and integrating their supporting systems and processes. They are achieving results by integrating cohesively, rather than instituting a series of individual process or functional area improvements.

One global consumer products company recently faced this exact problem. Complexity was rife, particularly among the company's European operations. Prior to adopting a business simplification program, the conglomerate's operations were disjointed, without a clear strategic focus. Part of this stemmed from the fact that over time the business had evolved from a series of country based operations, but the component parts had never fully integrated. A profusion of national brands generated high marketing costs, and a lack of ingredient and packaging standardization added to the complexity.

In response, the company began the task of wholesale transformation. Led by senior management, they drove a coordinated business simplification program across their worldwide operations. Their step-by-step program sought to narrow the company's focus to four primary categories, migrate national brands to pan-European and global brands, and sell and dispose of non-core businesses. In addition, the company decisively lowered the complexity of their manufacturing and distribution footprint by shifting to a focused-factory approach in which category-focused plants each supplied multiple markets around Europe.

Within five years, the company rationalized their manufacturing footprint from 14 country-based plants to three country-based centers of manufacturing. At the same time, they closed eight of 16 distribution facilities and increased their outsourcing distribution elsewhere around the globe. These changes simplified their global supply chain structure and succeeded in reducing changeover times, lowering manufacturing costs and improving asset utilization.

PUTTING THE SUPPLE IN SUPPLY CHAIN

Hau Lee, Professor of Operations, Information and Technology at Stanford Business School, remarked, "Great companies don't stick to the same supply networks when markets or strategies change. Rather, such organizations keep adapting their supply chains so they can adjust to changing needs. Adaptation can be tough, but it's critical in developing a supply chain that delivers a sustainable advantage."[75]

Competition

"The nature of competition is shifting away from the classic struggle between companies. The new competition is supply chain vs. supply chain." *Source: David Taylor, Supply Chains—A Manager's Guide.*

The best supply chains are dynamic, focused and flexible. In this lies competitive differentiation. The German company Siemens, for instance, is recognized for its supply chain excellence, both on a corporate level and in their subsidiaries, some of whom boast awards to this effect.

When the medical device unit, Siemens CT, was struggling in response to rising costs and tightening profit margins, the group rethought its whole mechanism for sourcing, building and distributing their specialized X-ray machines. To forge faster response times and greater organizational dexterity, Siemens CT flattened their management structure, aligned performance incentives against critical supply chain metrics, streamlined their external partnerships and adopted lean production techniques.

As a result, Siemens CT compressed the time it takes to build one of their specialized machines from 22 weeks to just two, making it easier for the company to ramp up or down production in the face of changing market demand. On-time deliveries also improved. What was a mediocre 60% on-time rate now stands at nearly 100%. Today, the company can deliver its product within a two-hour window, even when, as author David Taylor observed in studying the company, that window involves closing down a street and dragging in a giant crane. [76] Such reliability ties directly to customer satisfaction and burnishes a reputation for quality.

BMW CFO Stefan Krause views flexibility in the supply chain as a critical success factor. "Volatility," he says, "is a constant in any supply chain. The more rigid your business is, the less able you are to adapt."[77] The ability to provide flexibility is something Krause considers to be a key determinant in evaluating prospective partnerships, for both competitive as well as for risk management reasons. The more agile your supply chain, he stresses, the lower your risk exposure.

Stanford's Professor Lee would probably not be surprised to learn that adaptability and alignment were critical to Siemens CT's success. Lee has spent the last 15 years studying corporate supply chains to learn what works and what doesn't. In his highly regarded paper "The Triple-A Supply Chain," winner of a 2004 McKinsey award, Lee suggests that in contrast to traditional thinking, the twin goals of faster and cheaper do not by themselves create sustainable competitive advantage.

On the contrary, he asserts that supply chains dominated by a focus on those two characteristics tend to deteriorate over time. The more enduring supply chains in his view are anchored by three traits: agility, adaptability and alignment. These are Lee's Triple A's, and he believes evidence shows they combine to create the most defensible and enduring competitive position.

Armed with Lee's research, one is still faced with a practical design question. How do you bring these qualities to bear on the various links in one's chain, and, moreover, how do you begin to tackle the large and daunting challenge of transforming the supply chain?

For some companies, wholesale change works well. For others, gentle reform phased in over time is better. Either way, our experience shows it's best to consider which dimensions of the supply chain offer the greatest leverage. This is best accomplished when the potential impact of improvements is assessed along these four dimensions of value:

- ❏ Process, Technology and People
- ❏ Risks, Controls and Compliance
- ❏ Tax
- ❏ Financial Performance

Take tax, an oft forgotten element, for example. A recent KPMG International White Paper found that many companies are unaware of their tax planning strategy. Tax planning, more than any other financial function, tends to operate in isolation, not only from management and boards but also from other business units. One source indicated that just 14% of corporate tax departments had a tax strategy that had been approved at the board level.

This is unfortunate. Supply chain business solutions almost always generate tax consequences. In most cases, the resulting gains are significant and capable of enabling long-term results. Consider pairing the tax attributes of several different sourcing or supplier options to see which deliver the most optimal results. Whether income or transactional, managing tax costs appropriately can improve a company's overall supply chain efficiency.

Process, risk and financial performance improvements can be assessed in a similar manner as a means of establishing a rewired and stronger supply chain architecture. To a large degree in today's competitive environment, this means carefully assessing the strength, performance and value of one's sourcing arrangements.

SOURCING

Capital scarcity, the volatile M&A market, and the economic climate are exerting pressure on global business leaders to revitalize existing operations, broaden operating margins and foster greater earnings predictability. In light of this, the management of most multinationals are taking a cold, hard look at the processes they undertake in-house to see which non-core activities might more effectively be handled outside.

Some businesses have taken the lead and already source successfully. Companies such as Hewitt, Standard Chartered and British Airways, for example, each turn to human resources service providers for a range of payroll processing and recruitment assistance. British Telecom, Nokia and SAP rely on technology outsourcers for customized software development as well as hosting, maintenance and support. Maersk Sealand and Philips partner with operations providers to support order tracking, claims and credit card processing. The list goes on.

In all, companies source a broad mix of functions externally, in areas such as those listed in Table 2.

Table 2: Functions Companies Source Externally

Finance and Accounting	Manufacturing	Human Resources
Technology services	Logistics and operations	R&D and product design
Marketing and sales	Customer service	Product development

Source: © 2005 KPMG International

Tracing the Source

Among the first to tap into Asian sourcing partners, the computer industry serves as a microcosm for an increasingly sophisticated array of benefits. In the beginning, computer businesses turned to Asian affiliates mainly for low-skill, low-wage, high-volume manufacturing tasks. This procured an initial cost advantage to help inure them against the ravages of their intensely competitive market environment. Over time, these rote activities changed as companies sourced ever more complex and multifaceted tasks.

> *Modern Sourcing*
>
> Delivers high-level design work as well as manufacturing, inventory management and supply chain capabilities.

For example, while in the past many computer companies relied on outsourcers solely for assembly and component manufacturing, today they are expanding these relationships to include original design manufacturing, a capability once considered too complex and specialized to outsource. This allows these businesses to cluster component and capacity risk and standardize the design and production of high volume, low value parts.

Hewlett-Packard (HP), wanting to capitalize on its growing market share in digital cameras (a space dominated by Canon and Nikon) turned to Tekom, a Taiwanese company with experience in personal computer cameras. For HP, the

Tekom partnership represented more than simply an efficient mechanism to manage costs. It was also a means of strategically extending Tekom's PC camera experience to the field of digital photography.[78]

Sourcing Surge

The benefits enjoyed by the United States and Europe, the primary regions pursuing offshore sourcing, are considerable. On average, U.S. companies get a 40% return on every offshoring dollar spent. For example, compared to most American and European call centers, offshoring can save companies up to 50% in operational expenses. Savings extend to other industries as well. Catherine Mann, of the Institute of International Economics, found that the global sourcing of component parts lowered the cost of IT hardware from 10 to as much as 30% since 1995. The value derived from the globalization of IT services not only added to productivity but directly contributed 0.3 to U.S. GDP between 1995 and 2002.[79]

Triage

"The best companies I see are beginning to triage the supply chain. . . . They'll separate vendors that provide commodities from preferred suppliers that they have good relationships with from strategic suppliers that they create alliances with. They manage the supply base through those three different elements in very different ways, using different metrics, different processes, different people, and different mentalities." *Source: Interview with Robert Porter Lynch, Harvard Working Knowledge, September 8, 2003*

LEVERAGING THE SUPPLY CHAIN TO SECURE ADVANTAGED MARKET ACCESS

The surge in offshore sourcing stems not only from the wage differential that exists between the developed and developing worlds, but from an emergent talent differential as well. Asian universities turn out three times as many more engineering and science graduates than Europe and the United States.

This resident technological expertise is fostering localized best-of-breed status in certain IT disciplines, such as wireless technology and integrated circuit design. In turn, these distinct skill sets are leading to more refined supply chains.

Ravi Aron, Assistant Professor, Operations and Information Management, Wharton School, University of Pennsylvania, believes this evolution points towards a new type of economic organization—a hybrid between a company and a market. In his view, the unfolding sophistication of the sourcing and supply chain relationship enables company managers to operate "more like independent actors responding to market signals, and outside suppliers to behave more like corporate subsidiaries."[80]

John Hagel, former McKinsey partner and independent management consultant, would probably agree. In his experience assisting clients with supply chain issues, he has found that, "Employees of offshore manufacturing operations are often in a better position to evaluate the availability and responsiveness of suppliers, particularly where robust local 'ecosystems' of technology are developing."[81]

MANAGING SUPPLY CHAIN RISK

Supply chain sourcing is not a one-size-fits-all endeavor. Despite the many benefits, many sourcing arrangements fail to deliver the desired benefits. According to the National Outsourcing Association of the United Kingdom, anywhere from 20–25% of outsourcing relationships break down in any given two-year period, and 50% fail within five years.

Healthy Supply Chains

Deliver meaningful returns in the form of risk mitigation and performance improvement, allowing companies to capture the full business value of their extended supply chain.

The reasons for the poor track record vary. Among the potential stumbling blocks are a faulty sourcing strategy or inadequate implementation and support. In other cases, a service provider may simply not have the appropriate understanding of the business and its needs. Also common is a failure to achieve the benchmarked cost savings or quality levels that fall below expectations. In almost every case, failure is the result of poorly devised, badly negotiated and feebly executed sourcing arrangements.

Aside from the inevitable frustration such failures cause within the business, supply chain errors, whether in implementation or oversight, can create a considerable amount of business disruption and introduce damaging barriers to future sourcing efforts.

KPMG International encapsulates the range of potential risks as follows in Table 3.

Sourcing partnerships entered into without appropriate due diligence can ironically inject more cost into the supply chain than existed before. For example, inadequately controlled operational risks can lead to spiraling errors, wherein forecasts within the supply chain and at given outsource parties are inflated to provide a safety cushion. When these bloated forecasts are passed down the chain, a domino effect can ensue. Then when actual customer demand falls short, the whole system bears the margin losses caused by the excess inventory.

Companies may also underestimate the cost of long supply chains. China has been a popular sourcing destination, but

---

Table 3: Sourcing Risks

Strategic risks: Risks associated with the scenarios, plans, directives and decisions that define and integrate the resources and services required to fulfill the business objective.

Operational risks: Risks attributable to operational problems with service or product delivery or inability of an entity to recover fully and timely from unforeseen events.

Financial risks: Risks attributable to interest rate, foreign exchange rate movements, taxes or the entity's inability to meet payment obligations as and when they fall due.

Regulatory risks: Risks caused by violation of laws, rules, regulations, prescribed practices and ethical standards.

Technology risks: Risks relating to the failure of the outsourced entity's IT environment to effectively process and deliver products.

Reputation risks: Risk of negative publicity regarding business practices associated with the outsourced operation.

Source: © 2005 KPMG International

manufacturers that leap on the "China or bust" bandwagon because the cost structure seems so compelling may find themselves in trouble. Rather than advantaging the businesses, the blind pursuit of the low-cost manufacturing that China offers may prove harmful.

Whether China or some other emerging nation, the lowest cost country may not be the best solution for every company's sourcing strategy. Highly-customized products or stringent delivery timelines may compel a different approach, one where the supply chain is more closely located. As Andy Green, Chief Executive Officer, BT Global Services, observed at a 2005 World Economic Forum panel on the subject, automatically favoring the lowest bidder can lead to expensive mistakes. Instead, managers should always ask: "What is the long-term competitive advantage that will allow a vendor to do a particular job cheaper than us?"[82]

Finally, since the purpose of a good sourcing arrangement should be to allow the company to focus on higher value activities, the inability to reorganize efforts along these lines can potentially serve as the biggest weight on an otherwise effective arrangement. Particularly in first-time sourcing partnerships, leadership back home may find it hard to resist overmanaging the relationship. Instead of being free to focus on customer facing initiatives, they may unwittingly serve as another layer of supply chain management. While appropriate controls are necessary, so too. are appropriate levels of empowerment.

EXITING GRACEFULLY

Once a company has made a significant investment, whether in financial, personnel or other resources, it can be difficult to unwind on both a practical and psychological level. Yet, the banding and disbanding of supply chain components is a necessary aspect of a well-functioning system. An exit strategy and plan is essential when considering any large-scale initiative or transformation. Just as management and boards put in place a variety of business continuity and disaster recovery procedures to protect and backup key assets, the same contingency planning should be applied to strategic supply chain discussions.

A business enters into a supply chain arrangement with certain risk assumptions in mind. These give shape to important termination clauses and other contract protections. Still, any such provisions must be carefully evaluated to ensure they provide reasonable protections in the event of significant business changes on the part of the supplier, events such as management changes, regulatory or other financial noncompliance, labor disputes or political disruptions, all of which could jeopardize business functionality. In addition, companies should have a backdoor option in place in the event the supplier or sourcing partner fails to meet agreed-upon performance standards.

Sometimes however, the exit strategy is employed in support of a less extreme business case, namely the logic of profit and loss and basic good business sense. General Electric, for instance, was one of the first companies to explore offshoring.

Back in the 1990s, then CEO Jack Welch mandated what is known as the 70:70:70 rule. By that he meant that 70% of GE's non-core work would be outsourced, 70% of the outsourced work would be done offshore, and 70% of that offshore work would be performed in India.[83] The resulting entity, GE Capital International Services (GECIS) became the largest back-office processing employer in India, carrying out increasingly complex tasks such as auditing and financial analysis.

In the fall of 2004, however, GE sold the unit to a private equity group. This marked a big shift, but in a strategy becoming increasingly common, GE pulled out of the offshoring arrangement in favor of a more cost-beneficial outsourcing one.

Under the GECIS deal, GE will retain a smaller equity stake while continuing to use GECIS services under an outsourcing capacity. Moves such as these are occurring in large part as a means of reducing headaches that can ensue in managing a "captive" enterprise, challenges such as employee attrition, and local labor laws. As John Atkinson, head of Gavs Information Services, a back-office processing centre based at Chennai in southern India, observed, "When you move certain processes offshore to a country like India, your cost-savings are one-off—they tend to diminish pretty quickly."[84] By exiting its offshoring relationship in favor of a more practical and cost-efficient sourcing one, GE made its supply chain a better and stronger fit for its business.

In this way, good companies continually revisit the business basis behind their supply chain. In what direction are the best supply chains evolving? Let's look ahead.

LOOKING FORWARD—
THE TRANSFORMATIONAL SUPPLY CHAIN

A promising new area of supply chain exploration is emerging. Move over efficiency. The supply chains of the future, some of which are already being pioneered, will not only be adaptable, agile and aligned, they will be transformation agents to help capture and exploit unclaimed business value.

Companies practiced in the art and science of sourcing are turning to their supply chain for assistance in transforming the wider enterprise. For them the supply chain is becoming a change management tool, allowing the gentle piloting of an enterprise-level change initiative.

As they evolve, some partnerships will offer companies the opportunity to piggy back on the local market expertise of their sourcing relationships, reducing the distribution risk of expanding sales into less familiar regions. Others will provide for a sweeping overhaul of one's market positioning. Still others will allow entrée into a promising new product category, one that will strengthen their global business model. While these are some of the same reasons business leaders

Change of Focus

"As the corporate world wakes up to the potential the supply chain offers for substantially improved customer service and financial performance, the focus of many supply-chain departments has shifted from cost to customer offering, touching on the issue of 'brand' and cutting across functional boundaries and geographic territories."
Source: The Economist, March 7, 2002

turn to M&A, outsourcing is often a less tumultuous affair. As Jane Lindor of Accenture's Institute for Strategic Change observed in an interview with Harvard Business School, ". . . With outsourcing, you get a finer point on your pencil."[85]

The value of the supply chain as a transformation tool is that it lifts company eyes off the cost sheet to the horizon. Focus is trained on external results, like shareholder returns or and improved value proposition.[86]

CONCLUSION: A MORE KNOWLEDGEABLE SUPPLY CHAIN

The modern supply chain can be a source of critical competitive advantage for companies that leverage the links in the chain to support their global business objectives. In upgrading total supply chain performance, executives and managers may want to keep the following suggestions in mind.

Create a Value-based Supply Chain

The most sophisticated companies view their supply chains less as a means to an end and more the critical corporate artery for creating value. The more complex and weighty one's system, the greater the potential for value to be hidden, wasted or lost. The ability to simplify and more tightly align the supply chain in a way that responds to changing customer and market needs presents a company with a major competitive weapon.

Set a Differentiated Objective

Thoroughly plot what it is your business is expecting to gain from the relationship. Is it simply a cost advantage, or are you looking for your partners to add a distinctive skill-set, or entrée or expansion into a new geographic or product market? Different criteria will drive different styles of supply chain and sourcing relationships.

Chart Your Course

Secondly, check on the competition. What is their supply chain and sourcing approach? Is it working? Are there ways you can do it better? If your rival has a lock on the top Indian call-center partner, for instance, don't go for second best. Determine a way in which you can elevate customer satisfaction through a segmented call center or through other similarly strategic one-upmanship.

Get Inside Your Suppliers and Your Customers

With the competitive terrain assessed, be sure to conduct appropriate due diligence into your prospective partners' business practices. How do they buy? What is their inventory policy? How robust are their own supply chain partners? Are there critical gaps that may add volatility and cost to your business? Among other considerations, be sure you understand their projected cycle times and what contingencies and forecasting techniques they have in place to guard against swings in supply or demand.

Evaluate Continuously and Set New Objectives

Lastly, regularly evaluate the performance of your supply chain and the various sourcing components that may comprise it. Establish metrics around important quantitative and qualitative factions, such as internal and external customer and supplier collaboration. Determine if forecasting technologies are doing the job, or whether increased investment is needed. Then go back to your partners and hold the equivalent of an annual performance appraisal process. Address both the positive advances engendered by the deepening relationship as well as higher go-forward benchmarks that reflect the combination of your competitive assessment and customer need.

The Bottom Line . . .

Supply chain and sourcing relationships must be supple. Companies bound by less than optimally efficient systems create openings that competitors will be eager to spot and exploit. Supply chains are no longer merely another part of business infrastructure, but a competitive tool to be molded and maximized.

CHAPTER 6

Marketing With a Global Face

"If this business were split up, I would give you the land and bricks and mortar, and I would take the brands and trademarks, and I would fare better than you."

—John Stewart, Former CEO, Quaker

If the medium is the message, as the famous Marshall McLuhan saying goes, then today's consumer is spoilt for choice. Indeed, the global marketplace sports a profusion of products, brands, segments, media outlets, marketing channels and distribution vehicles to a degree previously unheralded. The vast array is a bonanza for consumers, but oftentimes befuddling to global marketing leaders who must steer a profitable and strategically-directed course through the melee.

Technology and improved global supply chains allow for greatly extended global reach and an ability to mass customize like never before. As sub-brands and line extensions grow, the

> **Brand Growth**
>
> "Roughly three-quarters of the Fortune 1000 consumer goods companies manage more than 100 brands each. From 1997 to 2001, the number of brands increased by 79 percent in the pharmaceutical industry, by 60 percent in white goods and travel and leisure, by 46 percent in the automotive industry, and by at least 15 percent in food, household goods, and beverages." *Source: McKinsey Quarterly, 2004, Number 4, McKinsey & Company.*

complexity and cost of building awareness among an increasingly distributed customer base has grown proportionately.

Before cable and satellite networks, the typical media buy was straightforward. Today, it is a different story. The advent of digital video recorders, such as TiVo, that allow consumers to bypass traditional television advertising, and the proliferation of viewing channels, have forced the advertising industry to reevaluate long-held practices.

Procter & Gamble CEO Jim Stengel jolted the media world when he announced in a speech before the American Association of Advertising Agencies in 2004 that, "... today's marketing model is broken. We're applying antiquated thinking and work systems to a new world of possibilities."[87] As *On The Media* later reported, "when the world's biggest advertiser, and therefore the world's biggest underwriter of media content, is looking elsewhere to spend its five and a half billion dollars a year, that makes Madison Avenue and Hollywood shudder."[88]

The effects go beyond advertising. The entire interconnected discipline of marketing is undergoing roiling change.

Chief marketing officers are grappling with a function and model that in many cases must be radically reformulated in order to improve both investment returns and global effectiveness.

GLOBAL IDENTITY IN FLUX

Corporate identity is based on perceptions, including such soft, but important qualities, as reputation and image. Companies try to direct those perceptions toward the positive attributes that underlie their products and services. But perceptions are also molded by the customer and employee experience.

If the identity one assumes is not sure-footed, brands may flounder. Yet, it can be hard to know what one's global identity is when the underlying nature of the business and its markets are themselves changing. Further challenges arise in ensuring that global affiliates understand and communicate the same personality, purpose and character.

Global competitiveness requires that companies articulate their global identity very clearly. Just as a parent encourages their children to develop individual potentials, they also hope to instill common core values, a shared family identity. Corporate identity management is similar. While foreign locations must reflect the sensibilities of the local markets they serve, the corporate mission, and ultimately the shareholder, is best served if the company's global identity is rooted in a common purpose and shared values.

Dr. Kenichi Ohmae, former managing director of McKinsey and Company in Japan, expressed it this way in his book, *The Borderless World*:

> "Maintaining a corporate identity in a global environment is different. . . . Formal systems and organizational structures can help, but only to the extent they nurture and support intangible ties. . . . Most important, however, is a system of values that all employees in all countries and regions unquestionably accept. A global company must be prepared to pull out of a region where its core values cannot be implemented."[89]

The ongoing human rights crisis in Sudan, for instance, led three Western oil companies, Sweden's Lundin Petroleum, Canada's Talisman and Austria's OMV, to pull out of the country and sell their oil stakes. The conditions in the Sudan simply made their participation in the country incompatible with their core values. Negative press reports and petitions from human rights groups were also a major factor.

Indeed, identity and the brands that are built around it, work best when they reflect the already strong motivations of their audiences. They must also reflect reality. And that reality must be one that global customers are willing to pay for. For this equation to succeed, the brand identity must be anchored on three pillars: it must be true; it must be distinct; and, it must be consistent.

A Pepsi bought in Beijing must taste the same as a Pepsi bought in Sydney. The core value, a consistently great tasting, high-quality product, makes the Pepsi brand resonant and strong. The wholesale membership club, Costco, likewise

Trust

"When your core values are black and white, then all the people in your company understand what's expected of them and you're that much closer to doing what you say you're going to do 100 percent of the time. That means you're that much closer to being a trusted brand." *Mike Moser, co-founder, Goldberg Moser O'Neill*

excels in its core business, selling discounted food and consumer goods. It makes no pretense of offering the widest variety of product, or offering the most compelling customer service. Those qualities are not part of the core brand. Its mission is clear and upfront and both employees and shareholders benefit accordingly.

The first step in any global remarshalling of corporate identity is to clarify for one's internal and external constituents just what principles define you, the ones for lack of which your company would falter. Then, get the word out. As part of a corporate rebranding campaign, the Taiwanese-based Acer Group invested significantly in employee outreach. They strongly believed that only through employees' genuine belief and exercise of the brand values would the company experience the true power of the brand. How well a company's value and offerings translate in another culture is another story.

THE MIRROR EFFECT

With one's identity etched and shared, the next task is communicating its value to the various markets in which one operates or hopes to operate.

Sometimes companies assume that what works in their home country will work in another. They take the same product, the same messaging, the same advertising campaign, even the same brand names and export them wholesale to the new market. The result in many cases is failure. Why? The assumption that one approach works everywhere fails to consider market differences, local competition, and varying degrees of economic sophistication and advancement. While some companies that sell internationally can be successful following a standardized marketing strategy, it is a mistake to assume this approach will work without sufficient research that addresses this question.

In the heyday of the Internet bubble, many companies raced to expand globally, often empowering field offices to create their local marketing presence as well as the look and feel of the local websites. For Avon cosmetics, the result was a lesson in brand extension they won't soon forget. While Avon's Japanese website featured an animated butterfly flitting across the page, the Venezuelan website showed a beautiful woman with a syringe, promoting the company's collagen product. In all, their 44 country websites each portrayed a different image and different message. There was no consistency. What did it say about Avon? Which messages were the right ones? Who could tell? The messaging was so indistinct. Certainly, few promoted the core brand values that Avon headquarters intended to drive.[90] While the strategy allowed Avon to build a rapid global presence, it failed to deliver a cohesive global brand.

Recognizing the confusing, and occasionally conflicting, brand messaging the various sites promoted, Avon responded. Today, the company boasts a unified brand across its global portfolio of websites. The lesson they learned was threefold: expand at a measured pace, maintain clear oversight and be consistent.

International Touch

"If you get the insight right, there will be a universal market and not just a rural or urban market." *Sanjiv Gupta, CEO, Coca-Cola India*

Global marketing is very much about bringing both consistency, as well as local market sensibilities, to bear on one's messaging and branding. It is about texturizing the core brand rather than inventing disparate personalities. Complex though it may be, global identity is chiefly about communicating the many facets of one character. There is one self, though the brand mirror can, should and does reflect many faces.

ACHIEVING THE RIGHT BALANCE

This philosophy sounds very well in theory, but how does one go about instituting it in practice? Core brand content should remain just that: core. Fundamental brand drivers need to be applied consistently throughout one's global footprint, even if the means through which they are expressed, whether visual or textual, differs. Other attributes can be localized. Although the precise ratio varies by industry, the general rule of thumb is a 70:30 mix. In extending one's brand across borders, retain 70% core content and customize the remaining 30%.[91] Intel, for example, applies a blended approach as part of their analysis in expanding into new markets. While they are careful to employ a local approach in every country, Arvind Sodhani, president of the company's venture capital unit, says they do look for universal attributes in their investment decision making as well as, importantly, the exit strategy should one be needed.

Texturizing a brand for local market conditions involves more than simply translating the language from, typically, English to the foreign tongue. Yet, surprisingly, this is what happens in too many cases. Consider the following examples:

❏ In 1996, Reebok discontinued a new line of women's athletic shoe called Incubus, a word referring to a demon that attacks women in their sleep.
❏ The Scandinavian vacuum manufacturer Electrolux used the following in a 1970s American advertising campaign: "Nothing sucks like an Electrolux."
❏ A Chinese company hoping to breakthrough to western markets translated its brand into "White Elephant Auto Parts."

> ### Oversight
> The chief marketing officer and team should manage the overall brand effort, while local in-country marketing managers should be engaged to help customize the remaining 30%.

EXTENDING THE UMBRELLA

Language issues aside, a distinction must be drawn between the global brand, the sub-brands and the messaging extensions that support them. Some companies find that one universal brand works well. Take FedEx, one of the most recognized brands in the world. After re-branding from Federal Express to FedEx in 1994 to support its global expansion, the company has been rigorous in using its FedEx name across its various services, even bringing well known, acquired brands, such as Kinko's and Viking Freight, under its FedEx manifold.

The use of a universal brand like FedEx serves two purposes. It builds recognition and awareness and it can enable significant cost savings. Consider the inverse. The popular stomach ulcer medication, Prilosec, goes variously under the names Prilosec in the United States and Canada, and Mopral, Gastroloc, Omepral and Antra in other countries. For such a global sector, the pharmaceutical industry has been relatively late in moving towards global branding strategies for its products.

Until recently, the widespread tendency was to give local operating companies the responsibility for brand interpretation. This can aid local market differentiation, but can be confusing, say, for an American tourist in Paris whose ulcer kicks in and whose local arrondissement pharmacist prescribes Mopral. As Edwin Colyer put it in his article for Brand Channel, "Hey . . . I'm not taking this. My family doctor always prescribes Prilosec and I know that works fine."[92]

The recognition factor in applying an integrated global brand is an important asset. So is the cost advantage. Global branding and shareholder value have a causal relationship according to most branding experts. A universal brand can reduce marketing costs and facilitate a faster, more consistent and more streamlined global launch.

It is not unusual for multinationals to rely on local advertising agencies to generate market-specific advertising and communications. Instead, by unifying under a common global brand, the company could shift the bulk of such work to its primary agency, thereby reducing the cost of customized marketing materials, as well as providing negotiation leverage with the primary agency for the volume work.[93]

Sometimes it is necessary to separate consumer perception of a brand away from the parent company, such that there is no natural association in the consumer's mind. This can be done for a variety of reasons. For instance, a company may have built its history selling "sensible" products at "sensible" prices, but now sees an opportunity to craft a new, higher-end product for an entirely different population: the luxury market. Separating the luxury brand from the parent's brand might pave the way for better acceptance among the desired audience. Not doing so, in fact, could injure the new brand and impact the marketing ROI.

For example, when Toyota introduced its first luxury line in 1989, it did so under a new brand, Lexus. Recognizing that it would be difficult to extend the public's perception of the Toyota brand, which at the time was known for being high quality, but not high end, it created an entirely separate identity for its new luxury model. The Lexus was launched as a "global premium brand for the 21st century" and marketed and sold separately. By separating its luxury brand from its mainstream models in this way, Toyota created a distinct and new market for its product. The strategy worked. Author Chester Dawson observed in his book *Lexus: The Relentless Pursuit* that "within two years of its introduction, Lexus overtook Mercedes-Benz for the crown of best-selling luxury import brand in the U.S. and had clinched top place in J.D. Power & Associates influential ratings for quality and service."[94]

A SEGMENTED GLOBAL MARKETING MODEL

Evidence suggests that profitable market expansions come when the multinational places financial performance first and tailors discrete marketing and operational plans accordingly. One of the most critical issues facing multinational companies operating in Asia, and particularly China, is their ability to serve the mass market cost-effectively, something at which local Chinese manufacturers have excelled.[95] Whereas umbrella brands generally work well for overall marketing purposes, diversified segment-specific brands tend to advance developing world performance best.

Diversify

While sound business strategy may support using one global brand, it is rarely sound strategy to have one global marketing plan.

For affluent customer segments, it might make sense for the business to employ a traditional marketing model, one that provides investment in high-end packaging, advertising and brand building. For the lower end of the market, however, the better performing companies shed these fineries. The goal, first and foremost, is margin enhancement and operational efficiency. In all likelihood, the farmer in rural China whose wardrobe is minimal, has no electricity and washes clothes with a washboard, is less interested in refined stain removal techniques and color sensitive washing agents than he is in a cheap and effective laundering detergent.

To serve this farmer in a cost efficient manner, the most successful companies emulate local market techniques. This can involve product reformulations, lower-end packaging, limited to no advertising, and a low-frills launch. It also generally means bringing in a local brand manager familiar with the competition, local regulations, manufacturing and production techniques. In many cases, it means renaming the product to avoid cannibalizing the premium end of the line. This approach salvages the bulk of core content, but adjusts the remaining marketing "recipe" to suit the tastes of its audience. The 70:30 principle is retained, and execution is more efficient.

The appropriate marketing mix takes stamina, involves risk and requires nerve. Success can be fleeting and failure expensive. To stick, the marketing mix must connect with the consumer's perception of the company and the brand. Since cultural contexts fluctuate, sometimes rapidly, enduring success is achieved when segmentation is tested, tweaked and retrained on a continuous basis.

SURVIVING AND THRIVING IN LIBERALIZING MARKETS

Brand marketing after economic reforms and market liberalization is an entirely different proposition than brand marketing in the open market, developed world.[96] Before India liberalized in 1985 and opened its economy in 1991, new product plans from competing companies were easy to unearth. That is because the government required everyone to submit them in detail in order to get industrial and import licenses. The information submitted could thus find its way into competitor hands. In addition, once a foreign direct investor succeeded in entering the country, sustaining market advantage was comparably simple since the entering company held a virtual monopoly. Today, it is a different story. While competitive plans are no longer as easy to get one's fingers on, the market also does not offer the comparatively easy victories it once did to foreign-owned companies.[97]

India's market liberalization opens promising opportunities for foreign manufacturers, but selling to open-market emerging countries is still risky territory for new market entrants. Achieving the right marketing mix takes time and typically requires a longer payback horizon. This can make some companies jittery, concerned about shareholder impact. Yet, those who engage for the long term can find their stamina rewarded.

Good Car-ma: Hyundai's Successful Experiment in India

This was the case with Hyundai Motor Company. Hyundai learned from studying the Indian marketplace that Indian consumers place a great deal of weight in calculating the lifetime ownership costs of a vehicle. In light of this, the company invested considerable time reconfiguring an extremely efficient car model that would require only reasonably priced and readily available spare parts over the course of its life.

Curb Appeal

"Photographing the new Hyundai Santro Xing turned out to be an inadvertent vox populi of sorts. We were inside the Phoenix High Street shopping complex in Mumbai . . . and witnessed an endless procession of people commenting on the car . . . I could park a Mercedes-Benz SL at that same spot and people would have admired it but walked on. . . . While you wouldn't touch anybody's SL, with the Xing, there was an entire 'touch and try' session taking place. Many of them were bold enough to open the doors and even check the upholstery . . ." *Srinivas Krishnan, Motoring Magazine, India*

This investment in understanding and catering to specific local custom paid off. Unlike most other multinational automotive companies that entered the Indian market in the 1990s, but let joint ventures do the manufacturing (many of whom would turn out to have limited financial resources), Hyundai established a fully-owned subsidiary and hired some of the most respected executives in the Indian automotive industry to run it. In addition, rather than importing manufacturing parts, which were more costly, Hyundai sought and found local supplies that could be used in the production of their locally built cars, thereby keeping costs in line with local competitors and, moreover, giving them a distinct cost advantage over other foreign-owned car companies.

"The very essence of Hyundai's strategy," reported *Business India*, "was to localize heavily from day one to give it a very early cost advantage, the number one priority in this highly price sensitive market."[98] When Hyundai entered the Indian market, no one had heard of them. Today, they are the country's largest automobile exporter, with annual sales in excess of 100,000 cars.[99]

Long-Term Gains

Whereas today there may be a limited market for certain complex or advanced-market products and services, such as insurance or mortgage banking, with education, product modification and time, a company may create a rich source of future opportunity. Just as Citibank created a new product and sizeable new market with its Suvidha account (see Chapter 2), so other companies and industries can tap into promising value sectors through education and "bridge" products.

For long-term-minded businesses that establish a personal presence, the rewards can be significant. McKinsey & Co analysis shows that of the more than 50 multinationals operating in India, nine market leaders, including British American Tobacco, Suzuki Motor, Hyundai Motor and Unilever, had a return on capital employed (ROCE) of 48%, 14% higher on average than the 26 companies that make up the next tier.[100]

General guidelines for surviving and thriving in liberalizing markets include:

- [ ] Segment and localize products and product marketing to reach fragmented audience and avoid cannibalizing premium or global brands.
- [ ] Recognize that even developing markets buy on perceived superior value, not just price alone.
- [ ] Adjust the supply chain to keep costs in line, tilting balance in favor of local parts and supplies.
- [ ] Retain significant ownership of local joint ventures to ensure control and that the right level of investment is maintained.
- [ ] Engage strong local management who know the market, the regulations and consumer tastes.

WHO OWNS THE MESSAGE?

That the classic global marketing model is undergoing a structural shift is undeniable. But, until now, ownership of the message has rested largely with the company, its advertising agencies and its public relations team. That, too, is changing. Just as the arrival of the Internet posed an enormous challenge and opportunity for brick and mortar entities grappling to understand its impact, today the spectacular growth in web logs, or blogs, threatens to unseat traditional marketing communications strategy.

The blog represents the latest frontier in viral marketing, on global proportions. For those not yet exposed to the medium, and that still includes most of us, a blog is an on-line journal consisting of linked articles, usually posted in reverse chronological order, written by "citizen journalists" and corporate executives alike. In fact, anyone can write or post to a blog; that's part of the charm. Blogs are often intertwined, linking to other blogs in domino fashion. There are political, corporate, hobby and pop culture blogs. The range is seemingly unending. Some blog posts can be ridiculous in the extreme. Still, others can be bitingly on point.

When Microsoft launched its blogging software, MSN Spaces, in December 2004, it probably didn't expect the site to be sent up one day later by the popular blog Boing Boing. The detailed and frankly humorous critique written by editor Xeni Jarden ricocheted around the Internet world, or blogosphere. Soon over 300 blogs were linked to her "Seven Dirty Blogs," some from around the world, but some also from influential and respected sources such as Dan Gillmor, former technology guru for Silicon Valley's *San Jose Mercury News*.[101]

While Microsoft may not have welcomed the negative reception to MSN Spaces, it did not shirk from acknowledging it. Rather than turning the matter over to its excellent corporate communications team, Microsoft called in a more powerful ally, a rank and file employee-turned Microsoft blogger named Robert Scoble.

The "Scobleizer," as he is known in the blogosphere, does not have a window office, but the view he provides Microsoft fans and detractors alike is peerless. The *Economist* calls him

Microsoft's Chief Humanizing Officer, and they may be onto something.

Scoble's response to the torrent of criticism raining down on MSN Spaces? He agreed.[102] Not only that, as a Microsoft employee and sanctioned blogger, Scoble made a point of acknowledging the early flaws of the software and indicated that he was sharing these with Microsoft's technical team. Scoble's commentary won Microsoft considerable respect and "street cred" and won Scoble, himself, minor celebrity status in the blog world.

That blogging is hot is an understatement. The *New York Times* reports that there are currently 10 million blogs. The *Ottawa Citizen* says there are 31.6 million.[103] The discrepancy is part of the surging blur that represents this fast-growing, real-time communication medium. This would be just another tech phenomenon except for one thing: it is unquestionably impacting the speed and nature with which global goods and services are being marketed.

The world's largest auto manufacturer, GM, may be going through a difficult period, but its Fast Lane blog has been a hands-down success. The site, which hosts topics ranging from product launches to business strategy, averages 4,000–5,000 hits per day from people around the world.[104] One of the keys to its success is the active presence of GM Vice Chairman Bob Lutz. The other is Lutz's willingness to post readers' negative jabs as well as his own insightful commentary. The reach of such powerful corporate blogs as Fast Lane are an advertiser's dream. An individual posting can receive between

50 and 300 return posts and be linked to a plethora of other sites. It is viral marketing at epidemic proportions.

Blogging and Global Identity

The scale and reach of blogging make it a rich prospect for companies with global marketing ambitions. Given the onus on the marketing function to be more exacting with its research and more statistical in its analysis, blogs offer a powerful means to test, vet and assess consumer reaction—and can do so, moreover, for very little corporate investment.

Blogs Get the Word to the World Fast

Bloggers covering the Tsunami tragedy in Southeast Asia were faster than traditional television media in posting photographs and news stories of the unfolding event.

The Fortune 500 are taking note. Giants like Procter & Gamble, McDonalds and Coca-Cola are already experimenting with what former McDonalds Chief Marketing Officer, Larry Light, christened "brand journalism," a layering of brand messaging of which traditional advertising will occupy a smaller part and new communication media a correspondingly larger one.

Smaller regional companies, particularly those in the developing world, are also availing themselves of the ready scale and networking that blogs afford. Asia is already home to a thriving network of blogs. To those who would fear the sales impact of product criticism, evidence suggests their fears may be overplayed. By and large, readers are discerning. They can filter obvious rants and acknowledge that while one aspect of the product may not be perfect, a balanced review can lead to that most compelling consumer benefit, "truth in advertising." Company honesty about good features and weaker ones actually lends it credibility, builds trust and draws buyers in.

Yet, to be effective, company sanctioned blogs need a sensible backbone. Determine first if your culture is tolerant of the open, honest communication that blogging demands. Will blogging expose your company to business or financial risks that you are not prepared to take? Are you willing to adequately staff and resource the blog? A dedicated internal blogger, or community of bloggers, who will keep the site fresh and current is essential. Most importantly, create an official corporate blogging policy, even if you do not maintain an official corporate blog. Let employees know what standards you expect them to keep, such as respect for corporate secrets and intellectual property. Finally, launch quietly. Give yourself the time and space to smooth any kinks away from the glare of public attention.

GLOBAL PORTFOLIO MANAGEMENT

With identity, branding, segmentation, emerging market issues and changing communication streams all being juggled, what must global marketing leaders do to bring oversight and management to these assets? While portfolio and investment discipline is fairly standard practice in other corporate functions, the same rigor has not typically been applied to the marketing function. Yet, with the heightened pressure on CEOs and CMOs to shave cost and enhance performance, that may be changing.

As consultants David Court, Jonathan Gordon and Jesko Perrey observed in the *McKinsey Quarterly*:

> "While all marketers track their progress, few measure it end to end by following the trail all the way from the effect of spending on a brand's drivers to the influence of those drivers on consumer loyalty and the influence of loyalty on revenues and margins and, finally, to the question of whether any increase in profits justifies the spending."[105]

To determine one's marketing ROI, the best analyses encompass the full range of hard and soft marketing activities, from advertising and sponsorships, to communications and support activities. This portfolio view helps management pinpoint the locus of competitive marketing leverage and identify investment opportunities with the greatest potential returns. As products, brands and channels proliferate, this synergy in aligning marketing investment with the most productive assets will prove differentiating.[106]

Getting a handle on the multifaceted and extremely layered world of marketing activities is no easy task, but technology is offering some assistance. Tools like marketing resource management and related software that track planning, budgets, forecasting, and production across a company's global enterprise are gaining traction among blue chip entities.

Companies like Merrill Lynch and NBC/Universal are embracing the technology to bring improved oversight and control to multi-country, budget sensitive, quick-turnaround production processes.

In the end, global managers that make the effort to map their marketing spend this way will be in the best position to:

- ❏ Identify their best performing practices.
- ❏ Determine where and how to modify or eliminate underperforming ones.
- ❏ Compare their spend and brand performance across borders.
- ❏ Examine country and regional performance on an equivalent basis.

By thoughtfully applying investment fundamentals to the marketing discipline, chief marketing officers will be better able to rise to the increasing pressure the function is under to show concrete ROI.

CONCLUSION

Corporate marketing groups have become de facto global organizations, with complex budgets, return-on-investment targets, management expectations, and an explosion of brands and products to deal with. Global marketing leaders are rising to the challenge to turn marketing into a corporate discipline with improved transparency and accountability in the boardroom. They are doing so by retuning their company's global identity, leveraging it into a consistent family of brands, and differentiating the manner in which far-flung global markets experience them.

The Right Voice

German Chancellor Willy Brandt once said, "If I'm selling, I speak your language. If I am buying, dann müssen Sie Deutsch sprechen." (Then you speak mine.) *Source: CMO Magazine, Donald DePalma*

In tapping their distributed global customer base, chief marketing officers and their teams are becoming adept at segmentation, engaging local-market brand managers to better emulate low-cost competitors and tailoring bottom-of-the-pyramid market entry practices. They are relying on technology to take them to the new frontier of global communications, via blogging, as well as to more traveled statistical ground, via resource management tools. Increasingly, they are bringing formal portfolio management discipline to bear to justify and prioritize their global marketing investment.

In all, it is a convulsive, but exciting, time for marketing organizations as they man the front lines of global competition for the companies they serve.

CHAPTER 7

Global Value Creation

The only sustainable competitive advantage is to learn faster than the competition.

—Arie de Geus, Dutch writer, author of *The Living Company*

Be not the first by whom the new are tried, goes the age-worn adage. In keeping with that spirit, Wal-Mart, though the most sizeable retailer, was not the first major one to make inroads in Asia. Others, like Sears, Kmart and Target all laid down extended supply chains in the region before them. But the delay on Wal-Mart's part was purposeful. As a retired senior Wal-Mart executive explained to *Frontline*, "In going to Asia and then into China, department stores always beat us. A lot of people were there long before we were. But it was part of the strategy to let them go through the initial tortures. [Wal-Mart would] step in when all the groundwork had been laid."[107]

When Wal-Mart subsequently arrived on the continent, they benefited from an Asian manufacturing base that was already well trained by their predecessors in how to produce goods for the American consumer. They lost no time exploiting the intellectual capital and leveraged that learning curve with the continual pursuit of low-cost, high-efficiency production.

Wal-Mart's success comes from its rigorous way of squeezing value from its enterprise. By not rushing the market, by making sure that the economics of global expansion complement the underlying business model, and by exploiting the girth of its knowledge assets across its worldwide footprint, Wal-Mart maximizes the yield from going global. That same discipline can be replicated by others who make understanding their company's value continuum an embedded way of doing business.

Toyota, which aims to achieve 15% of global share, has staked a considerable part of its strategy on its ability to sell its products globally. Its success is built on its ability to join its reputation for quality with an emerging track record based on innovation. Already, its investment in energy-efficient hybrid models, such as the Prius and the upscale Lexus hybrid, have been huge market successes. It is a strategy that is making some of its European competitors, who have long prided themselves as being the industry's innovation leaders, nervous.

THE VALUE CONTINUUM

In the face of unpredictable market forces, all businesses, large or small, need a clear path to increasing cash flow and a clear means of guarding against unwanted exposure. Qualitative and quantitative measures may account for total value, but the ability to translate this value effectively to the bottom line most concerns a company's stakeholders.

Businesses constantly adapt in the pursuit of value, molding and remolding core processes to the needs of their stakeholders. The best *preserve* value through consistently superior service; they *create* value by leveraging intangible assets and proactively exceeding stakeholder expectations, and they *release* value through carefully adapting their organization to take advantage of regional market differences. In this way, thriving businesses offer investors the full measure of their company's worth.

Fundamental value comes from the wedding together of focused strategy, continual innovation, effective processes and talented people wrapped up with exceptional leadership, execution and integrity across the enterprise. Together, these form a company's value continuum. To achieve excellence in the corporate value continuum, however, one must understand how the business creates value, in other words, how it is positioned to address the following:

Mapping the Value Creation Process

1. What factors contribute the most value across the global organization?
2. How do those factors connect to the underlying business, domestically and abroad?

3. What processes optimize value creation between asset classes? How do they drive business performance and profitability? What geographic issues affect that balance?
4. What global relationships are most responsible for driving value? How can these be best measured, managed and leveraged?
5. How do we measure, govern, leverage and protect our intellectual capital across our worldwide business?

Multinational companies and those aspiring to operate in foreign markets have a special obligation in mapping their value creation process. The reach, breadth and complexity of their assets, intellectual and otherwise, offer huge opportunities to preserve and create value and an even larger responsibility to ensure none is left on the table, unrecognized and unused. This is another way in which Intel Corporation leverages its in-house venture capital group. For instance, in tracking exactly these types of opportunities, the company recently announced the creation of a $200 million Intel Capital China Technology Fund. For Intel's stakeholders, China is as Sodhani describes it, "a force for technology innovation in the worldwide marketplace," and one the company believes will be intrinsic to its value creation process.[108]

THE VALUE CREATION PROCESS

Customer feedback, industry analyses, competitor and market benchmarking, performance measurement and related analytics provide useful direction with respect to understanding those factors that drive optimal value for the business and its operating units. Established companies employ a menu of these and related options as part of their strategic planning discipline. Connecting the dots and understanding how those factors tie to the underlying business is a more complex matter. Too often, subjective inclination can take the place of active due diligence.

While a value proposition may be clear, the value creation pathways that support it are often not well mapped, nor sufficiently comprehensive. That can make it difficult to spot interdependent processes and synergies that create fundamental value. Even when profit migration is well understood, pathways need to be recalibrated regularly against the undulating needs of the business. Otherwise, long-held practices thought to be accretive to value can go unchallenged, and new, leading practices overlooked. In the absence of careful modeling, the surge of a hot business trend, such as offshoring and outsourcing, can risk sweeping even the most disciplined manager in its tow, pushing aside their customary care and business case analysis to determine if that approach is right for them.

Kim Perdikou, U.S. CIO of the Fortune 1000 company Juniper Networks, understands the discipline required of the value creation process. In an interview with *CIO Asia*, Perdikou stressed that securing an optimal return on investment is a major challenge for any global organization. At Juniper, for instance, they "scrutinize every potential project according to the value it would provide to the business, and we do it in conjunction with the business leaders."[109] If the project does not map to Juniper's strategic goals and does not impact their key performance indicators, the company won't do it. Juniper is equally serious about the need to perform regular value map reassessments, something Perdikou describes as "spring cleaning." "Most people," she says, "implement systems and can never work out if they are a success or not. We make it a point to look at the usage and success of every application each year. And if they are not delivering value to the business, we switch them off."[110]

With the intensity of global competition increasing the penalties for flawed judgment and poor execution, companies that commit senior resources to an annual evaluation of the value creation process and its supporting capabilities will be inherently more competitive. This will be a defining competency for enduring global businesses.

Matsushita is similarly disciplined. The company has set an aggressive goal of attaining an operating profit to sales ratio of at least 10% by the year 2010. Matsushita president, Kunio Nakamura, admits that, "Many people were stunned when they heard this." However, he stresses, "I am convinced that the role of the head office is to represent shareholders and their interests." To do that, he believes, "We must be uncompromisingly selective in choosing the growth areas and prioritize accordingly."[111] One of the ways Matsushita seeks to deliver on this promise is to withdraw from those businesses and activities that fail to reach the 10% operating profit ratio in the long run.

Nakamura explains, "Sales do not matter." Instead, he says that what matters are, "cash flow and a positive Capital Cost

Management (CCM) index." CCM is Matsushita's own metric, created by leadership to emphasize return on capital. A positive CCM means that the return on invested capital meets the minimum return expected by shareholders. In this way, Matsushita not only talks about delivering value, but they have anchored their entire business around generating it and hold themselves accountable to shareholder specific metrics.

As companies build out their global strategy, the best will examine their value creation processes across two fronts: how to optimize and *position* value across their global enterprise, and how to optimize and *release* the value of their intangible assets.

GLOBAL POSITIONING—OPTIMIZING VALUE ACROSS THE GLOBAL ENTERPRISE

A study by management consultancy Bain & Co, assessed the performance of 7,500 publicly traded companies from across seven countries over a period of five years, from 1996–2000. What they learned surprised them. After screening the original pool of 7,500 along various metrics covering financial health, years established and so forth, Bain narrowed the list down to the 729 best performing. Of that group of 729 companies surveyed, only one-sixth (124) grew foreign sales and operating profits faster than their domestic rate. In many cases, this was despite heavy investment in global expansion. What went wrong with their value chain?

There are many pitfalls on the path to global prosperity. Some companies in the Bain study expanded too rapidly, sometimes without evidence of adequate returns. Others, in

their haste to enter new markets, failed to perform appropriate local market analysis, and did not properly understand
their competitors and customers, leading to waste, miscues
and other errors. Still others neglected to develop a repeat-
able market entry strategy, forcing them to bear the financial
burden of continually reinventing their approach. Finally,
many companies overlooked the criticality of hiring local
managerial expertise (see Chapter Six) and relied too heavily
on expatriates.[112]

A value chain is no good if it is strung with loose ends and
knots. Indeed, it is hard to channel the heft of an organization
when the parts that hold it together are poorly aligned. Things
become unhinged. By contrast, the best performing companies only expand beyond their borders when the business case
for doing so is so persuasive there is no other choice, and only
after they first demonstrate mastery of their core business. As
consultants James Root and John Smith observed:

> "Building a strong core business requires a management
> team to fully understand the boundaries that delineate the
> business, recognizing clearly which customers, costs and ge-
> ographies are part of the core, and which are not. Through
> that lens, they see global expansion neither as an essential ex-
> tension of their core or as a growth option to be evaluated
> alongside other opportunities. Foreign norms and local mar-
> ket knowledge are important—but not as critical, it turns out,
> as having a well-honed system for making money at home.
> In fact, 'going global' will mislead companies that have not
> first understood the profit dynamics of their industry."[113]

The results of a well-articulated global plan can be significant.

BMW: "DRIVING" GLOBAL VALUE[114]

The BMW Group has developed a deliberate, anti-cyclical approach for entering new markets. They do so by taking what CFO Krause calls, "a series of small but sustainable steps." The first of these typically tests the waters by working through importers. This confers two useful advantages. First, it provides BMW with needed local market expertise to support the group's own learning curve. Second, Krause says, "It spreads the entrepreneurial risk burden across several shoulders."

If this initial foray offers strong evidence of long-term growth potential, BMW gets involved more directly, establishing subsidiaries to provide a solid foundation for the company's market presence. Krause believes the establishment of an in-country subsidiary network is critically important to the enhancement of the brand profile. In fact, as he notes, BMW Group was the first foreign automotive manufacturer to operate a subsidiary in Japan and in Korea, moves he believes directly contributed to the brand's success in those markets even during the Asian economic downturn at the beginning of the century. As Krause emphasizes, "Anti-cyclical action is a key feature of a long-term market development strategy." Today, the BMW Group operates six wholly-owned subsidiaries throughout Asia, including new subsidiaries in Thailand, Indonesia and the Philippines. In addition, if high import duties restrict further development of the market and retail increases are only possible through local added value, the BMW Group opens an assembly plant. There, pre-manufactured parts and components from the company's German plants are assembled by locals on the ground. The BMW Group currently has assembly plants, through its partnership network, in Russia, Egypt, Malaysia, Indonesia and Thailand.

As a final step, Krause studies opportunities to establish fully-fledged production locations in the most important regions, according to the belief that "production follows the market." This is a strategy that brought the group huge success, even in costlier markets like the U.S. "Since opening our assembly plant in Spartenburg, South Carolina in 1992," says Krause, "sales of the BMW brand in the U.S. have almost quintupled," success he credits in large part to BMW's in-country investment and commitment. In 2003, the company also established a production and sales joint venture in China, in order to fully exploit the enormous potential of this booming market.

The BMW story offers one illustration of the way in which disciplined attention to the core business and its supporting value creating processes can pay strong dividends.

GLOBAL APPROACH

Determining whether a company's value map justifies global expansion is one thing; figuring out how best to expand is another. There is no one strategy nor one right solution. The industry one company competes in, its economic and cultural profile, stage of development, and other company-specific variables all factor into the final analysis.

Home-Based

Some businesses, particularly those whose product or service requires a high degree of specialization, such as pharmaceuticals or telecommunications, may generate the greatest value for their stakeholders by sticking close to home. By clustering research activities together, some R&D driven enterprises can derive potentially better synergies. In addition, businesses that rely on highly-customized, low-volume goods may require sophisticated assemblage that is better managed near the entity's geographic center to achieve necessary efficiencies and preserve desired margins.

While few models are adopted in the absolute, businesses such as these often sell and market abroad, while retaining their main production muscle at home. Where the business case justifies more significant global manufacturing expansion, these companies tend to pursue it by way of acquisition or joint venture, buying or partnering with a local market leader equipped with its own locally-based production and distribution capabilities.

Verizon, the top-ranked telecommunications company on *Fortune's* "Global Most Admired" list, is the largest telephone and wireless operator in the United States. It is also a major global player with 33 million international customers. Yet, the company's operations are largely U.S.-driven. Its profitable expansion is generated by way of select global partnerships and investments, which allow it to maintain a significant global presence without the cost, logistical and regulatory hazards of exporting a massive telecommunications infrastructure abroad. Verizon maintains active investments in Americas-based telecommunications companies and operates in Europe through its successful joint venture with Vodafone. In this fashion, Verizon leverages value from the global marketplace by building on the strengths of its core business.

Regionally-Based

Other businesses generate optimal value by establishing regional beachheads. These entities service major regions of the globe on a more-or-less self-sufficient basis. A company's European center, for example, may manufacture and sell to Europeans from within Europe, to Asians from within Asia, and so forth. These units can link to shared services hubs located elsewhere, but tend to bundle and distribute the majority of their other services in-region. Degrees of localization vary, of course, depending on the size of the area in question as well as cultural variances.

This model is understandably popular among people-based services businesses for whom familiarity and access to the local or regional market is a critical differentiator. Many consulting firms and financial services business operate in this fashion, usually supported by strong national offices in major locations. Versions of the approach are gainfully employed by logistics and transport businesses as well. Most airline, shipping and delivery businesses operate through hubs. Indeed, FedEx's hub-based system is one of the critical success factors behind its famed speed and reliability and a major contributor of value.

World-Based

A third direction consists of globalizing the entire business. Like a jigsaw puzzle, one's global footprint is put together by locating functions, operations and processes in the market that is able to add the most value, either through the lowest cost, the best distribution, the most efficient supply chain, or other metric. In this way, a discrete process such as customer service may be outsourced to India, component manufacturing may be run from Taiwan, and marketing may be managed out of regional centers. These entities base their global strategy on highly-efficient global networks and use cost and quality metrics to guide decision making with respect to where to locate a given corporate function.[115]

The world's largest construction and mining equipment company, Caterpillar, Inc., offers a fine example of global integration. For nearly a century, the heavy equipment manufacturer has been building infrastructure around the world. In fact, more than half of all Caterpillar's sales in 2004 were to customers outside of the United States.

The company's current structure reflects careful positioning and a finely-honed architecture. Shared services are located in the UK, Switzerland, Asia and the U.S., while products and components are manufactured in over 100 locations across 23 countries. A well-regarded global dealer network augments this infrastructure, offering rental services through more than 1,400 outlets worldwide, and providing financing and insurance for its dealers and customers.

That the structure is complex, there is no doubt, but neither is the fact that this highly tailored global enterprise generates outstanding value. The company's share price has nearly tripled in four years, sustaining strong growth even during the recent broader economic downturn.

Optimizing Value Across the Global Enterprise

Although some companies may function entirely in the context of a home-based, regional-based or world-based operator, most are a hybrid with companies deploying a combination of strategies. Some may have a regional structure for sales and marketing, while back-office and manufacturing functions are globally based. Hewlett-Packard for example, maintains three geographic headquarters, in the Americas, Europe and Asia, beachheads for its regional sales and marketing activities, shared services and administration. Yet, the company also manages product development and manufacturing sites in several dozen discrete locations around the world.

Whatever calculus a company uses in determining their ideal global structure, the common denominator must be value driven. In optimizing the value of their global enterprise, the best companies ground their approach on the strength of their core business and extend their reach only after justifying how the new markets will advance specific business aims. Going global is something many companies can do. Succeeding globally is a far different matter.

REALIZING VALUE GLOBALLY—OPTIMIZING INTANGIBLE ASSET VALUE

Intrinsic to any discussion of global value creation is understanding and exploiting the nature of one's global assets, a portfolio that today is based more than ever on the intangible. In a brand-driven, knowledge-based marketplace, the ability to identify, manage and leverage one's intellectual capital (its technologies, patents, processes, human expertise, brand, and so forth) is fast becoming a differentiator for global competitors.

Until the late 1970s and early 1980s, tangible assets drove the bulk of company value. That value was easy enough to assess just by looking at the balance sheet, which by and large offered a fair representation of a company's worth. The advent of the Information Age changed all of that.

IP Value

"Over 80 percent of [UK] investors say that the presence and quality of a company's IP strategy contributes to their valuation, and nearly 90 percent say that it contributes to their investment decision." *U.S. law firm Howrey LLP*

An examination of 3,500 companies for MIT's Sloan Management Review revealed that while book value accounted for about 95% of market value in 1978, that percentage shrank dramatically over the following two decades, falling to a mere 28% in 1998.[116] Today, intangibles make up the preponderance of company market value, particularly in knowledge sectors such as high technology, the life sciences and services.

Intangibles run counter to traditional economic principles. There is no depreciation. Intellectual property doesn't wear out. Unlike a hard asset, the more you use it, the greater the return. Intangibles can be mined and shared indefinitely, often with no incremental cost. Used well, they confer product differentiation, strengthen business relationships, protect pricing strategies, and offer potential for revenue generation.

Valuing the Intangible

Capturing, translating and reporting on the value of these assets have proven nearly as ethereal as the underlying intangibles themselves. One element of the valuation puzzle is the fact that intangibles run the gamut of the non-physical world, covering both legally-protected assets, such as trademarks and copyrights, as well as non-legal assets, such as knowledge, relationships and productivity.

> ### Tools Needed to Value and Visualize
> "The knowledge economy is therefore in the need of new management methods and techniques to identify the assets delivering most value, to visualizing how these resources drive performance and tools to measure and value the dynamic interactions of these assets."
> *Source: Cranfield School of Management, UK*

Baruch Lev, an accounting professor at New York University's Stern School of Business, is one of the foremost leaders in this area. His research into "information asymmetry"—

the gap between what is known about an information asset (brands, patents, R&D) and what is reported—indicates that a company's market valuation often fails to reflect the full value of its investment in intangibles. As a consequence, a company's share price may be undervalued and companies may be paying a higher cost of capital than they otherwise would.

Better reporting is one response to this issue. With the adoption of Statement of Financial Accounting Standards (SFAS) 141 and 142 in the U.S., companies involved in a business combination must now separate intangible assets on the balance sheet into discrete categories so they can be better seen and understood. A study of the effectiveness of the standards confirms a decrease in analyst forecast errors for companies involved in merger and acquisition activity based on the improved clarity of reporting.[117]

The new International Financial Reporting Standards (IFRS) have similar provisions. Under IFRS 3, companies undergoing a business combination may no longer pool them under the goodwill catchall, but must report on them separately.

In 2003 and 2004, the UK communications giant Vodafone booked goodwill charges resulting in record losses of more than US$9 billion. The company subsequently stated, in February 2005, that had it reported under IFRS, its profit for the six months to 30 September 2004 would have been greater by US$7.3 billion than under UK GAAP, as a result of the changed treatment of goodwill and intangibles.[118]

Not all intangibles are as hard to value. Among the most fungible is the company's brand. *Business Week's 2005 Global Brand Scoreboard* (see next page) illustrates just how powerful, and measurable, some global brands are The values, as noted, can be eye-popping.

When one considers the staggering dollar impact of Coca-Cola's ubiquitous red and white logo, the literal value of "Intel inside," or the effect of BMW's zealous focus on nurturing a premium brand, the intangible seems a little less ethereal and its value a lot more real.

Leveraging and Capturing the Intangible

While all may concede their importance, many fail to harness the full power of their intellectual assets. One study determined that 67% of U.S. companies own technology they fail to exploit. This represents the unwitting loss of millions of dollars. Unleashing that stored intellectual property (IP) can translate directly to improved shareholder value.

IBM, for instance, has over 40,000 patents. According to the United States Patent and Trademark Office, IBM has earned more U.S. patents than any other company, but until the mid 1990s, many sat around unused.[120] Once IBM began tapping its IP base more thoroughly, it witnessed an increase

2005 Brand Rank	2004 Brand Rank	2003 Brand Rank	2002 Brand Rank	2001 Brand Rank	Brand Name	Parent Company	Country	2005 Brand Value ($Mil)	2004 Brand Value ($Mil)	Change in Brand Value (%)
1	1	1	1	1	Coca-Cola	Coca-Cola	U.S.	67,525	67,394	0
2	2	2	2	2	Microsoft	Microsoft	U.S.	59,941	61,372	−2
3	3	3	3	3	IBM	International Business Machines Corporation	U.S.	53,376	53,791	−1
4	4	4	4	4	GE	GE	U.S.	46,996	44,111	7
5	5	5	5	6	Intel	Intel	U.S.	35,588	33,499	6
6	8	6	6	5	Nokia	Nokia	Finland	26,452	24,041	10
7	6	7	7	7	Disney	Walt Disney Company	U.S.	26,441	27,113	−2
8	7	8	8	9	McDonald's	McDonald's Corporation	U.S.	26,014	25,001	4
9	9	11	12	14	Toyota	Toyota Motor Corporation	Japan	24,837	22,673	10
10	10	9	9	11	Marlboro	Altria Group	U.S.	21,189	22,128	−4
11	11	10	10	12	Mercedes-Benz	DaimlerChrysler AG	Germany	20,006	21,331	−6
12	13	NR	NR	NR	Citi	Citigroup	U.S.	19,967	19,971	0
13	12	12	14	15	Hewlett-Packard	Hewlett-Packard	U.S.	18,866	20,978	−10
14	14	15	15	17	American Express	American Express	U.S.	18,559	17,683	5
15	15	16	19	18	Gillette	Gillette	U.S.	17,534	16,723	5
16	17	19	20	22	BMW	Bayerische Motoren Werke AG	Germany	17,126	15,886	8
17	16	17	16	NR	Cisco	Cisco	U.S.	16,592	15,948	4
18	44	45	41	38	Louis Vuitton	LVMH Moët Hennessy Louis Vuitton	France	16,077	NA	NA
19	18	18	18	21	Honda	Honda	Japan	15,788	14,874	6
20	21	NR	34	42	Samsung	Samsung	S. Korea	14,956	12,553	19

Source: BusinessWeek 2005.[119]

in patent royalty income from US$30 million in 1990 to US$1 billion in 2000. Today, their patent management model is viewed as best-in-class by other companies wishing to extract the maximum value out of their IP investments.

Companies derive competitive differentiation from their intellectual property in a variety of ways. Among them are:

Enabling new business models—Intellectual property can serve as the basis for dramatic changes in a company's business model. For example, the fabless semiconductor sector has risen in strength compared to the traditional, vertically integrated semiconductor company. They use their fabless structure to license valuable IP to chip manufacturers, sparing themselves the cost of managing such plants in what is a very cyclical industry.

Joint ventures and alliances—Some companies may have promising technologies that fall outside of their core activities. In these instances, a joint venture or alliance may be a smart way to leverage and extract otherwise dormant IP. BMW has used its joint venture network to underpin a vibrant growth strategy. It partners with other automobile manufacturers, such as Toyota, as well as a range of traditional suppliers, high-tech companies, energy supply companies, research laboratories, and universities. These alliances allow the car company to maximize R&D while lowering its spending and its risk.

Licensing—As demonstrated, large companies can have vast patent portfolios, a portion of which may be lying fallow. Licensing this unused technology can confer tangible benefits. IBM holds more patents than almost any other company in the world. By licensing some of their unneeded technologies, Big Blue generates over US$1 billion annually. In addition to generating revenues, licensing can also help a company advertise its expertise and, in some cases, generate new markets for technologies that it can later exploit.

Sale, Spinout or Securitization —In lieu of licensing, a company may decide to simply sell off its IP. What one company cannot use, another can. By digging into its patent portfolio in the early 1990s, for instance, Dow Chemical recouped US$50 million of investment cost in tax and administrative benefits from selling and donating unwanted patents. With better scrutiny and oversight of their patent portfolio, Dow grew its licensing revenue from US$25 million in 1994 to approximately US$100 million annually today. Indeed, the wealth of patents created in the 1990s high-tech boom has created a sub-industry of consulting businesses, such as Intellectual Ventures, run by former Microsoft Chief Technology Officer, Nathan Myhrvold, designed to help companies monetize their intellectual property.

Donating IP or placing it in the Public Domain—If a company is no longer interested in supporting a given set of IP, it may wish to donate it to a non-profit research institution or university. DuPont chose this route by using its polymer research to foster deeper connections with research universities and government labs and thereby broaden its global network of basic R&D sources.

To succeed in any of these efforts, a company must be able to access and order their IP portfolio. Yet, a KPMG study found that over 25% of companies have no provision for IP ownership in their employment contracts; over 70% have no performance metrics for IP; and, 50% leave IP outside the scope of internal audit, and have no IP reporting requirement to the board.

In light of this, leading practices are emerging. To reap maximum value from their intangible investments, business managers may wish to consider these six steps:

❏ Establish a comprehensive, enterprise-wide IP asset inventory.
❏ Obtain a thorough valuation of the IP portfolio.
❏ Develop integrated IP management strategies and policies.
❏ Assign ownership and accountability for management of the IP portfolio.
❏ Create appropriate performance metrics to determine optimal usage of the IP assets and regular portfolio reviews to determine if an asset should be leveraged differently, licensed, or sold.
❏ Prioritize the asset portfolio and the necessary protections around it.

A variety of compliance programs exist to safeguard and enforce IP protections. This function is well established within certain sectors like the entertainment industry, where license rights have long been a material component of the business model, but less so in others. For these it is important to develop consistent criteria over which IP should be protected and with how strong a lock. As with the underlying assets, the protections that surround them also need to be prioritized along cost-benefit lines. There is no point spending US$1 million on IP worth US$250K.

Where self-reporting among third parties is common, companies need appropriate assurance over those relationships and regular audits to check compliance. Where rights are breached, companies also need effective enforcement provisions to recover the loss and safeguard other assets.

In Sum: Optimizing Intangible Asset Value

The businesses that capture the available and untapped potential of their intangibles will reap the most benefit from their innovation, go farthest in ensuring their business is better appraised and understood, and harness the greatest amount of value for their stakeholders.

PUTTING IT ALL TOGETHER

Enduring businesses are constantly adapting in the pursuit of value. The companies that best achieve this continuously orient their business around the evolving needs of their key stakeholders. Mindful of resource efficiency and synergy, the best companies map their value creation process holistically. Before expanding beyond their borders, they first make sure they demonstrate mastery of their core business at home. Coupled with a disciplined approach to their global value positioning, these businesses also seek to exploit the untapped potential of their intellectual property portfolio. In this way, the value of their innovation and distinctive knowledge is captured and utilized.

Value creation is every executive's mission. With global competition squeezing profit margins, there is no room for inefficiency and even less tolerance for error. Striking the right asset balance in your corporate portfolio is as important as discipline, rigor and restraint. The best led companies groom these qualities into their organizational culture. In doing so, they reward their stakeholders with a proven value continuum and a value-based global strategy.

CHAPTER 8

Governing Change

"The true role of strategy is to describe a future worth creating—and then to reap the competitive advantage of preparing for it and making it happen."

—Pierre Wack,
former head of Global Planning, Royal Dutch Shell

To win in a global business depends critically on a company's ability to be a world leader in leveraging compliance, risk management and strategy in the generation of value. This demands unflagging commitment from management and the board of directors. Careful oversight requires meeting today's regulatory guidelines, while also shepherding the organizational response to new forms of enterprise risk.

Cash value-added, the cash flow return on investment, economic profit and total shareholder return are key metrics in measuring corporate value. They, in tandem with strong compliance and risk management, provide a structural basis for guiding global strategy. Yet, that strategy must be built on a detailed understanding of a plausible future. Our volatile global marketplace will inevitably yield new risks, new opportunities, and new sources of value that become apparent only after diligent study and application.

Those that treat planning as a regular, continuous activity will be in the strongest physical condition to survive and thrive in the future. Point-in-time reviews will never be able to sustain the onslaught of change, and corporate risk management and compliance efforts will suffer the consequences. Scenario planning, rolling forecasts, and regular early-warning monitoring are but a few ways to help companies achieve the continuity of planning they need.

This chapter looks at a few aspects to governing change from the top: compliance with the current regulatory environment and emerging global risks, and effective scenario planning to reduce future uncertainties and aid informed decision making.

COMPLIANCE

The last several years witnessed a nearly unprecedented level of compliance focus on the part of multinational companies everywhere, an effort catalyzed by the demise of Enron and related corporate ethics scandals. The passage of Sarbanes-Oxley, Basel II, and the impact of the new International Financial Reporting Standards have dramatically changed the control environment in many public companies, and nearly all agree that this has been for the better.[121]

> *Performance Benefit*
>
> "Compliance regimes are forcing companies to adopt formal busi-
> ness processes and reporting so they now have an opportunity to
> spot inefficiencies, overlaps and duplications of effort." *Adrian
> Wright, Managing Director, Secoda Risk Management, and former head of
> IT security at Reuters Group*

Barclays Bank provides just one example. Lindsay Nicolle
of Britain's *ComputerWeekly.com* reports that over the past
five years Barclays has spent 40% of its information technology (IT) budget on regulatory compliance, an enormous
sum by any measure. Barclays has used the spend to consol-
idate IT, centralize processing and improve standardization.
Though arduous in the doing, the bank today credits the
compliance push for generating £500 million in cost savings
and for improving the quality of management decision
making.[122]

A survey of 222 financial executives by Oversight Systems
found that 74% believed that their company benefited from
compliance with Sarbanes-Oxley and, of those, 33% said that
compliance lessened their risk of financial fraud.[123] Despite
these advances, many CEOs and boards concede the enormous organizational strain exacted by Sarbanes-Oxley compliance, the initial implementation of which exhausted the
time and resources of thousands of corporate employees. With
that phase largely complete, business leaders face a new challenge, namely finding a way to generate a return on the ongoing compliance effort, particularly when most surveys put its

average cost at between US$1.6 million and US$4.4 million annually.[124] Larger companies pay even more. Dave Burritt, VP and CFO of Caterpillar Inc., for instance, states that Sarbanes-Oxley compliance cost the company $30 million, $20 million in redeployed resources and $10 million in out-of-pocket costs.

The global aspect of regulatory compliance presents another challenge. While knowledge of domestic rules and regulations is one thing, translating that to a broader understanding of foreign regulatory requirements can be daunting. Operating in the global marketplace with its labyrinthine laws on the macro level, and myriad internal policies on the micro business unit level, requires time and mastery on the part of the organization.

Codes of conduct, control standards and policies may be etched, but global implementation of those standards takes time. As governance reform spreads to Europe and other parts of the world from its scandal-jarred epicenter in the United States, the result will hopefully spur greater harmonization of control standards and financial reporting.

Given all of this, the crux of the issue becomes how best to sustain the strong shareholder benefits of global compliance while also increasing the business return on investment. KPMG firms' experience shows that extracting value from the compliance process is a multi-faceted endeavor. As organizations mature in their ability to inculcate ongoing compliance, they typically progress through four stages of development. The KPMG International report *The Compliance Journey* describes them this way:[125]

In the *fragmented state* compliance is siloed and project driven. The effort to achieve compliance during this stage requires considerable coordination to connect disparate efforts throughout the enterprise.

With experience, the compliance effort evolves to a *functional state* that is program-driven. Here, accountability is assigned to a centralized compliance function that coordinates work streams across the enterprise.

From there, compliance can be elevated into an *integrated state.* At this point, the business starts to drive compliance. The organization ties programs to processes, giving business owners, rather than the compliance function, the opportunity to share oversight responsibility.

Over time, led by and owned by the business, compliance becomes an *embedded state.* It is enmeshed in the organization's culture. Accountability is shared by individuals and imbued in their day-to-day actions. In this stage of maturity, companies become the most disciplined and responsive to change. Governing change with respect to compliance thereby becomes not a once-a-year event, but an every-day event.

Getting through these stages requires committed leadership. In response, participants during the 2005 World Economic Forum called for "a more demanding boardroom."

Many of these participants, directors themselves, recognize the need for boards to take more active responsibility for challenging management assumptions, engaging in vigorous risk management oversight, and participating more knowledgeably and directly in shaping company strategy.[126]

A panel of 17 leaders and several dozen participants representing the Global Fortune 500 and premier universities recommended four steps for effective board oversight over compliance.[127]

Effective Board Oversight over Compliance

1. Board members should become more active in corporate planning and executive decision making.
2. Audit issues should be the sole purview of the audit committee, freeing remaining board members to focus on other issues of strategic importance.
3. A dedicated group should be considered to focus on possible operating exposures, relieving both the audit committee and board from this critical, but time consuming, activity.
4. The board should enforce the highest ethical standards throughout the company.

These recommendations, though heavy in their demands, seek to work-level the serious responsibilities carried by the board, allowing them to create specific groups of subject matter expertise and better execute on their oversight commitments.

BEYOND COMPLIANCE: EMERGING RISKS

Beyond the need to extract higher performance and effective management of compliance risk, today's leaders continue to manage other dimensions of enterprise risk. Today that means the strategic and financial implications of political upheavals, pollution, currency volatility and a wide stable of other variables.

Geopolitical volatility, for instance, has increased the potential for oil price shocks. This elevates the cost of doing business for fuel-dependent industries, such as airlines and plastics. It also injects new vulnerabilities for recovering economies, such as Japan's, where Victoria Marklew, a senior international economist for Northern Trust, worried that, "rising local oil prices in Japan will take a bite out of Japanese corporate profits just as profits are starting up again."[128]

Rising interest rates in the developed world, the large trade imbalance in the United States, the resetting of China's currency, and related economic factors place pressure on corporate treasury departments to find appropriate mechanisms to balance their risk exposure. Financial derivatives are one tool, but not all risks can be traded and not all are insurable.

Risk management today encompasses new areas beyond the traditional finance discipline. These can have significant bottom-line consequences. A supply-chain malfunction in

Taiwan may be an operational snafu, but it has immediate financial ramifications in today's just-in-time manufacturing world.

The menu of risks changes daily. Executives must gauge the likelihood of a collapse in real estate values (given analyst warnings about a possible global real estate bubble), assess their company's exposure to Kyoto protocol controls, and consider how best to protect access to vital natural resources in the event of environmental impact or outright closure. Indeed, *The Economist* notes that Asian carmakers and others who ply the Panama Canal regularly insure against the losses that would ensue should the Canal be inoperative.[129]

Kunio Nakamura, president of Matsushita, told us that, "the ability to predict and foresee risk is the most critical factor in risk management."[130] Those who fail to do so, he added, will suffer. In light of this, Nakamura created Matsushita's Global and Group Risk Management Committee. This committee, which functions as part of the company's hybrid risk-management structure, serves as an enterprise-wide risk oversight board. The group integrates and evaluates risk information collected from the risk-management committees of each of the company's global businesses and regional headquarters and formulates appropriate countermeasures. This structure allows the company to act swiftly and cohesively. Nakamura asserts, "If we are threatened by risks, we shrink. We should not be afraid of risks. Instead, we must concentrate on preventing the most damaging and optimizing the rest."

The complexities of global financial management can be dizzying, their array clearly diverse. Yet, consider the price of failure:

RISKS AND THEIR POTENTIAL CONSEQUENCES

Risk	Potential Consequences
Reduced Market Confidence	• Degradation in debt rating • Higher directors' and officers' insurance premiums and reduction in insurance coverage • Lessened ability to attract board members and potential suitors
Reduced Investor Confidence	• Decreased market capitalization • Eroded demand for equities • Decreased analysts' ratings
Reduced Business Performance	• Increased management focus on compliance issues vs. business opportunities • Increased attrition and turnover • Decreased ability to attract talent

Source: KPMG International, 2005.[131]

RISK TOLERANCE

As these emerging risks indicate, ongoing compliance and risk management will evolve over time with the addition of new and changing business processes. With it comes the question of just how much risk a company is willing to take. What is the risk tolerance? As with any such measure, the right balance must be struck. The pressure for monitoring that balance and ensuring that the compliance effort meets the test of improved transparency, reliability and accountability rests with the board and upper level management.

Just as individuals have differing levels of risk tolerance, so do companies and industries. A startup probably has a larger appetite for risk than a publicly listed company, the high tech sector probably more than the financial services one. Their strategy and compliance needs to adjust accordingly.

Risk "Averse"

"A 2002 survey by McKinsey and the newsletter *Directorship* showed that 36 percent of participating directors felt they didn't fully understand the major risks their businesses faced. An additional 24 percent said their board processes for overseeing risk management were ineffective, and 19 percent said their boards had no processes." *McKinsey Quarterly, September 2003*

Boards, management and employees in any given entity must understand their company's specific risk appetite and the tolerance bounds around it. For example, does a recommended strategy create undue geographical concentration for the business? If so, how can that risk be transferred or mitigated? Can it be diversified, hedged, sold, insured against? What is the optimal risk treatment? Governance quality improves when the risk profile of the company is mapped and contingencies defined. Ultimately, the board determines where in the value chain risk should be tolerated or reduced.

From there, governance requires recognition of ownership. Who owns and drives specific elements of the strategy? Who owns and drives specific elements of compliance? And, who owns the responsibility for specific elements of risk management? The answers to these questions are not simple, but without them accountability is hard to demonstrate.

Good boards oversee not only compliance, but also performance, recognizing that both impact on the risk, and ultimately the reward, are borne by the company. "Don't waste a crisis," was the message from Cristóbal Conde, President and Chief Executive Officer, Sungard, USA, another participant at the 2005 Davos conference. Instead, he advised, spend half your time addressing the problem and use the other half to develop on the opportunities that it creates. In keeping with that spirit, the risk management processes that guide strong stewardship can directly affect the company's ability to generate long-term financial value.

FORESIGHT

Governing change is everyone's responsibility, from the top on down. Yet, to govern change, one must, of course, know the direction in which it is blowing. This is where foresight comes in.

All businesses plan and some do it better than others. At its narrowest, some companies consider the financial plan to *be* the strategic plan. In that context, the strategist looks at the numbers and says, "Here is where we are today. Here is our projection. Now let's manage the gap." Though that method does serve financial planning purposes well, it does little to protect the company from an unexpected event that crashes in from the periphery. Good strategic plans are far more robust. And good global plans quite simply need to be.

Established multinationals can and do engage in multiple types of forward planning, nearly all of them sophisticated. How else to manage the intricacies of a thriving global enterprise? Real options modeling, econometrics, multivariable regression, forecasting and other quantitative techniques comprise just a few available tools in the planning arsenal. Together, they combine with industry and market intelligence to help craft the framework of an organization's strategy.

Desired points of competitive differentiation are tied to needed process improvements. Desired operating efficiencies are tied to process synergies.

Multivariable analyses such as these get a workout when extended to the complex and interdependent global market environment, but by keeping the business grounded on the drivers and sources of core value, the business can hone internal decision making, better deploy existing capital, and make smarter investment decisions. In this way, improvements in fundamental value can lead to improvements in shareholder value.

THINKING THE UNTHINKABLE

This ability to steer a business intelligently through an ever-changing future ranks high on an executive's wishlist.

Still, some leaders and some companies have shown there are ways to presage important global impacts on a business without possessing a crystal ball.

The art of scenario planning is one of the most effective, if among the most intensive, strategic planning methods available. Scenario planning is a means of learning about the future by studying and understanding the major driving forces shaping it. It is a formal methodology with roots in military intelligence and decades of practical business application now behind it. In an era with so much global uncertainty, scenario planning may thresh the wheat of the plausible from the chaff of the unknowable.

Royal Dutch Shell is credited by many for pioneering the field of scenario planning in the early 1970s. They have been modeling contingencies ever since. With valuable pipelines and resources dispersed throughout the globe, Shell views the careful evaluation of geo-political and economic risk to be a business necessity.

Shell's immersion began under the tutelage of Pierre Wack, a French oil executive with a penchant for mysticism and musing "what if?" As head of Global Planning for Shell, Wack realized that traditional decision-making methods relied too heavily on extrapolating the future from the present. The reality, he observed, is that so often the future sidesteps it altogether.

In light of this, what Shell needed was a way of seeing those forces that were likely to shape the horizon. Although Wack understood that the future is by definition indeterminate, he also understood that it is not necessarily unknowable. What if, he pondered, one were to search for and identify those "tendences lourdes" or driving forces that seemed most assured and articulate a future based on them? Then, Wack felt, you might have a radical, but insightful, base upon which to form educated decisions about the future.

This is the discipline that Pierre Wack brought to Shell. Through it, Shell was among the first to predict the coming dominance of OPEC and the likelihood of an impending energy crisis.

Shell Game

Wack's successor, Peter Schwartz, "identified Mikhail Gorbachev—not even a politburo member at that time—as a reformer who would lead the Soviet Union through sweeping changes. While the rest of the West was stunned in 1989 by the sudden fall of communism in that region, Shell was wondering why the process had taken so long." *FastCompany, Issue 60, July 2002*

Back in 1971 and 1972, Wack and his team realized that the United States was running out of oil reserves. At the same time, they observed that the American appetite for oil was rising steadily. To this unfolding supply/demand dilemma, Wack and his team teased out the emerging influence of the Organization of Petroleum Exporting Countries (OPEC). They perceived early on the considerable probability that OPEC nations might realize there was more value to keeping oil in the ground than drilling for it. If you control the supply, you control the price.[132]

From this analysis, Wack and his Global Planning team drafted two scenarios. The first took a business-as-usual look at the future wherein prices would remain stable. The second painted an altogether different world, one shaped by an oil price crisis that placed Shell's oil fields at risk of takeover and threatened the entire industry's growth.[133]

By drawing out the ramifications of each scenario, Wack's team helped Shell management perceive the nature of evolving world forces and "feel" its possible effects. This enabled management to imagine the set of the decisions they would have to make in the event any of those possibilities emerged. Thus, when the OPEC oil embargo did strike in October 1973, prompting a worldwide energy crisis, Shell was virtually the only energy business prepared to act quickly.

Shell is credited with using scenario planning to foresee a number of other world events, such as the 1986 collapse of the oil market, the fall of communism in the Soviet Union, the rise of radical Muslim jihadi, and the twin forces of globalization and liberalization. Today, it firmly credits the technique for enabling it to move from being one of the smallest of the seven major oil companies to becoming one of the largest and most profitable.[134]

Leading Practice

Others, including AstraZeneca, Fuji Photo and Visa International have used the discipline to good effect—AstraZeneca to retool its strategic planning, Fuji Photo to seize competitive advantage in the consumer digital camera market, and Visa to weigh the threat posed by peer-to-peer payment schemes.[135] 3M is another practitioner. They have applied the technique to great success in retooling the way in which they approach and communicate their business planning.

The public sector, too, has seen value. Scenario planning is viewed to have played an important part in South Africa's peaceful transition from apartheid to a stable multiracial government.[136] And for the past six years, America's Central Intelligence Agency (CIA) has partnered with the scenario planning firm Global Business Network (comprised of many former Shell staffers) in mapping certain aspects of the future.

ROOM TO GO

Still, despite the prowess of leading businesses such as these, the practice of scenario planning itself does not appear to be all that widespread. Scholars Chris Zook and Darrell Rigby observed that scenario planning "ranked 17th out of 25 techniques, with only 30% of senior executives in the Fortune 500 companies indicating that they had made use of scenario planning in 2000."[137]

The economic fallout that rattled the high technology and other industries at the turn of the century provides one indication of the inadequacy of some companies' planning processes. Indeed, hindsight reveals that far too many business plans were narrowly trained on meeting targeted financial metrics of interest to investors and analysts without due consideration of underlying risk factors and changes in the global economy and marketplace.

Has industry learned the planning lessons from the dot-com meltdown? It's unclear. A 2002 survey on the global pharmaceutical industry shows there is some room to go. One study of 100 companies, conducted by Fuld-Gilad-Herring Academy of Competitive Intelligence, found that "although 77 percent [of respondents] say their companies anticipate an increased level of business risk in the next two or three years, only 2.6 percent claim to have a formal early warning process in place."[138] Findings from the Hackett Group suggest a more widespread pattern across industry lines. They observed that, "Nearly half of all companies treat planning as a strictly fiscal and annual exercise, leaving them unprepared to deal with sudden, non-financial types of risk or catastrophe."[139] Their *2004 Best Practices of World-Class Performers* report instead remarks that, "world-class companies closely align strategic and tactical plans, enabling functional areas to contribute more effectively to overall business goals." This weakness exposes affected businesses and their stakeholders to shocks that might be better mitigated with a heavier planning commitment.

WE'VE GOT IT COVERED

One reason for the inadequate planning coverage is that many companies believe they already have a sufficient handle on near-term priorities. Long-term analysis, the type required of diligent scenario planning, looks five to 10 years out, too far out in the opinion of many to be of practical benefit. The demands of quarterly earnings announcements, the pressure to meet analyst expectations and the drive to show improved share price performance combine to skew planning orientation to the immediate future.

For example, a large pharmaceutical company with a history of tremendously successful medicines found itself caught off guard by the impact of biotechnology. Although the biotech phenomenon had been some decades in the making, the big pharmaceutical had declined to make the long-term investment and so found itself with a gap in its portfolio when the field exploded onto the market. This hole led the company to purchase a big-name brand at an equivalently large premium in order to secure a stake in that corner of the market. A more studied and long-term-minded approach to strategic planning might have spotted the impact of biotech earlier and allowed the company to enter or buy at a more advantageous time and price.

Another reason for ineffective planning is the tendency for most of us to extrapolate a future based on our own experience. It's hard to conceive a mental map of a world that lies beyond our perception. We are encouraged to "think outside the box," but certain ways of doing business become categorized, often subconsciously, as *the* way of doing business, and so go unchallenged.

The music industry, for example, was clearly unprepared for the assault of MP3 technologies and the spread of file sharing. Their whole business model was so tightly aligned to a relatively fixed CD pricing and distribution mechanism that the full frontal explosion of peer-to-peer file sharing challenged the historical structure of the industry. Yet, the surge in digital music was entirely predictable. After all, the Internet phenomenon was digitizing just about everything in sight, text, sound, and image, the quality of which was constantly improving and the cost of which was shrinking. That should have lit up the music industry's radar screen far earlier than it did.

That is the value of hindsight. Because a vast structural change to one's otherwise secure industry is so hard to contextualize, management may be at a loss to know how to act on it.

THE PROCESS

Effective scenario planners recognize this dilemma. They know their job is not to come up with the best scenario, but rather foster the best decision-making. The intent is not to predict the future, but to offer participants the opportunity to make more informed choices based on a deep understanding about the nature and shape of future business conditions.

The task begins by identifying what key question the analysis should address. If the question is fairly narrow or the variables involved few, other strategic planning or modeling methods may be preferable. Scenario planning, with its long generation time, is best saved for the really big "what ifs."

Next, the team should determine which decision makers among management the analysis should support. Far-ranging analysis is likely to impact diverse groups within the company. As early as possible, the universe of possible "readers" should be identified and to the extent appropriate, consulted for subject matter expertise. Shell and others often reach outside their walls on an as-needs basis for other forms of particular expertise.

The team then turns to the art of identifying those trends that seem most probable, those factors that seem most assured. Brainstorming as a group deepens the range of possibilities and sheds light on the impact these driving forces might have on the business. Scoping, researching, and ultimately prioritizing the list of uncertainties is a rigorous and intensive process.

Key drivers are mapped according to their degree of certainty and their degree of impact on the business. After the sifting is done, only the most influential, but least predictable forces should remain. They must also be plausible and consistent (one can't rule the other out, for example).

Storytelling

"Stories, together with the work getting there have the dual purpose of increasing the knowledge of the business environment and widen both the receiver's and participant's perception of possible future events." *Strategist, Martin Börjesson*

The scenarios are then defined and the stories written. The ones that emerge might take known certainties about today, population, climate change data, and the recent surge in European Muslim fundamentalism for example, and blend them with predictable uncertainties about tomorrow, such as renewable energy reaching a critical mass or the impact of a more deadly avian flu pandemic.

Stories are used for their intrinsic ability to illuminate possibilities that more formal planning methods may obscure. 3M, for instance, uses them to communicate their business planning in three ways.

As MIT's Leigh Hafrey observed, the first is in drawing new paths to success. Stories have the ability to capture imagination and shine light on previously unconsidered possibilities. Another advantage is the way in which stories encourage planning clarity. All stories require logic to hold them together and that requirement forces a certain rigor on the planning team. Finally, 3M values stories for their ability to inspire and motivate. They allow the reader to feel like they are part of the action, which can help an employee visualize their role and contribution. [140]

CONCLUSION: OVERSEEING CHANGE

Today's boards recognize the importance of active participation in strategy review, their need to challenge assumptions, ask critical questions and guard against unwanted exposure. They, along with all employees, must work together to create a strategically adaptable organization that responds quickly to changing market opportunities. That future is most successfully reached when their commitment, communication, and conviction come together under the mantle of leadership.

Sarbanes-Oxley, the Basel accords and other compliance activities present managers with streams of data. The most nimble companies will use their improved control environment as a lens through which to improve process performance. These business leaders and their boards will understand that the risks they take and the responses they make all impact the nature and scale of global corporate investment, and the structure of their global asset portfolio. As such, their strategic plan will document not only the path to value accretion but also the key risks.

Governing change involves linking the optimization of compliance, risk and strategy into the day-to-day operations of the business. This can only be done with top-level support and commitment. Board members and senior executives are the governors general of their corporations. They are responsible for overseeing the strategic direction of the business, ensuring appropriate accountability and, above all, for providing superb stewardship.

As stewards, their imprint shapes organizational ethics and sets the tone at the top, the overall quality of which can determine how much an organization pays to borrow money, its ability to attract and retain key resources and partners, and ultimately the premium investors will pay for an organization's shares. Governance and value, both moral and financial, are thus inextricably tied.

CHAPTER 9

Commercial Diplomacy

"We all want to go toward a bigger place than self-interest . . . the flow of natural human activity is about trying to understand the larger world."

—Yo Yo Ma, Renowned Cellist

O ver history, big industry has been accused of trampling on poor nations to mine their rich natural resources, leaving a wake of poverty, pollution, and general unhappiness in their wake. This was the fear when Exxon Mobil began construction of a mammoth 660 mile pipeline stretching from Chad in Central Africa to the Cameroonian coast. Even as the deal was being negotiated, rumblings of discontent were sounding among non-governmental organizations, (NGOs) such as Greenpeace and Friends of the Earth, who were predictably worried about the environmental impact. The governments of Chad and Cameroon also voiced concerns. After all, they wanted to make certain they received their fair share of the proceeds. International political bodies echoed skepticism over the promised benefits of the deal, recalling all too well the impact of similar oil projects by other companies in Nigeria and Sudan, projects they felt contributed to the political instability and strife that affects those nations even today. They expressed concerns about the sincerity of Idriss Deby, Chad president and a former general, criticized by many in the international community for his repressive regime, over his promises to repatriate the majority of oil proceeds to impoverished local communities.

This clamorous setting did not make for an auspicious start. But Exxon was no stranger to meeting resistance at its pipeline projects. Experienced though they were, it was nevertheless apparent that something novel would have to be done in this case. As Jerry Useem, a senior writer at *Fortune* magazine, described in his article for the periodical, "the Chad-Cameroon project seemed to meet all the preconditions for disaster. . ."[141] Recognizing that only careful negotiation could succeed in responding to the myriad and often conflicting interests involved, Exxon reached out to an independent intermediary to broker the deal. In a bold demonstration of commercial diplomacy at its cleverest, Exxon brought in the World Bank. Useem described it this way:

> "It was, even Exxon's critics concede, a brilliant tactical move. In keeping with its mission of alleviating poverty, the World Bank would lend $93 million to the governments of Chad and Cameroon so they could participate as equity investors in the project. But the Bank's real value extended far beyond that. By standing between Exxon and

its worst critics, on the one hand, and between Exxon and the troublesome host governments on the other, it could serve as a moral buffer, providing Exxon with invaluable political insurance." [142]

The strategy paid off. The project went through, complete with a jumble of concessions to the various interest groups involved, and the pipeline was inaugurated in October 2003. Chad has received approximately US$200 million in revenues from 2003 to the second quarter of 2005. Although the World Bank and other international bodies are still not pleased with the level of transparency the Chadian government is providing around their use of oil revenues, it is expected that over the next 25 years, Chad will receive upwards of US$5 billion in returned revenue from the first three pipeline developments.

> ### Diplomacy
>
> At the heart of efforts to build business in global settings is commercial diplomacy—the creation and enhancement of commercial relations between companies, or their representatives, and the governments, policy making bodies, regulators, and political agencies in established or developing global markets.

As for Exxon, the deal helped the company secure a more solid footing in this oil rich region. Exxon's 2004 Annual Report indicates the company's African holdings now account for 13% of total upstream earnings, with the Chad pipeline responsible for delivering 200,000 barrels a day. Former prime minister of Chad, Nassour Ouaidou, called the deal "the opportunity of the century."[143] It is clear, however, that without serious and deliberate commercial diplomacy, the pipeline never would have gotten off the ground, much less into it.

As the Exxon story demonstrates, as business becomes more global, the dynamics of international deal-making and diplomacy grow increasingly intertwined. In light of its imprint on global competitiveness, this chapter discusses the significance of commercial diplomacy and presents suggestions for improving the odds of success in cross-border negotiation.

COMMERCIAL DIPLOMACY: BUILDING BUSINESS BY BUILDING BRIDGES

Just as the art of diplomacy seeks to navigate national interests on a global scale, commercial diplomacy seeks to do the same for individual business concerns. This skill, whether oblique or defined, is increasingly in demand for business and government leaders alike. Teaming across boundaries in today's global marketplace means grooming managers with the capacity to create mutually beneficial relationships and partnerships. It also means providing them with on-the-ground experience to work with parties of influence, be they foreign companies, governments, policy makers, regulators or local organizations.

Such diplomacy is often considered a by-product of ascension up the corporate ladder, but the subtleties of successful international commercial diplomacy are not always acquired by accruing experience in the field. For many, the skills must be learned. In doing so, it is important to stress one key aspect of today's geopolitical and marketplace dynamics, namely the criticality of strong global relationships and the fundamental leadership requirement to build (and rebuild) the bridges that tie them together. Whether the object under construction is new business, new markets, new infrastructure or new policy, relationships form the foundation of nearly every business initiative, the health and welfare of which require active diplomacy.

LOOK BEFORE YOU LEAP

Diplomacy and deal-making go hand-in-glove. The most experienced international negotiators look not only at their own hand in a given deal, but also analyze the broader commercial interests at stake. They consider the economic impact of alternative policy options. They identify the interests of all possible stakeholders and note their political influence. They assess the local political climate and determine what interdependencies, if any, exist between national policies and their own commercial interests. They do this so that they might know and better understand just whom they are dealing with.

Yet even seasoned business leaders can come face-to-face with crucial diplomatic issues in commerce for which they may not have adequate insight. Anyone conducting business or planning to conduct business in China, for example, should recognize that they will have to work with the Chinese government at some point during the process. The lack of an appropriate mechanism to interact with Chinese policy makers may lead to a company's missing out on enormously valuable opportunities. Likewise, simply exporting strategies that have proven successful in one's domestic market can spell disaster when applied in unfamiliar global markets or in the markets of emerging nations.

Steps to Successful International Negotiation

With that in mind, experienced practitioners recommend careful consideration of the following factors, which if taken together can improve the chances for successfully negotiating a cross-border transaction.

In helping global and regional field managers navigate the complexities of a foreign business environment, it is important to:

- ❑ Know whom you're dealing with.
- ❑ Not rush the relationship.
- ❑ Use teams to assist in conflict resolution and evangelize the objective.
- ❑ Become versed in cultural deal-making preferences.
- ❑ Understand the nature and likelihood of government intervention.
- ❑ Adhere to strong ethical guidelines.

KNOW WHOM YOU'RE DEALING WITH

It goes without saying that when preparing to enter a new market or negotiate a transaction, it is important to know who the dealmakers are. This is because those parties may not be the ones sitting across the table from you. Like a bride or groom preparing to marry, one must meet the family and recognize the network of important relationships that hold important influence over the company you are negotiating with.

This is particularly true in nations where the judiciary and legal systems are weak. In these instances, there may be important legislative, tribal, corporate and community interests whose relative power and influence may have important consequences on your deal. Going into such a market without first understanding who may really be pulling the strings behind the scenes can be perilous.

Professor James Sebenius of the Harvard Business School calls such relationships "webs of influence."[144] He describes the experience of the U.S. company Stone Container Corporation. When Stone Container was negotiating a large forestry project in Honduras, the company's executives arranged to meet with the Honduran president and appropriate ministries who they assumed had the power and authority to approve the deal. While the president did indeed have the legal authority and ultimately approved it, they failed to realize that by dealing solely with him, they opened a hornet's nest in the process.

Had they prepared better beforehand, they would have understood that the Honduran presidency was relatively fragile, that the country had a checkered history working with U.S. multinationals, and that the exclusionary nature of the negotiating process raised suspicions within the Honduran

Congress, labor unions, political parties, potential competitors and other interest groups.

As a consequence, the deal became mired in controversy.[145] The deal-making process derailed while Stone met and worked with these various groups, backtracking to explain their project and intent and alleviate fears of corruption. Had Stone anticipated these concerns, they could have developed a more thoughtful initial presentation that would have assuaged these groups up front and avoided the adversarial process that ensued.

Do Your Homework

That preparation is essential is common sense. Yet like many sensible things, sometimes it is overlooked. Take the story of an American company that acquired a French affiliate. As *Time* magazine columnist Andrew Rosenbaum detailed in Harvard's *Working Knowledge* newsletter, to celebrate the deal the American executives flew to France and invited their French colleagues to lunch. The French were members of the business elite, having attended the '*Sciences Po'*, *Insead*, or other *grandes ecoles*.[146] They were accustomed to sophisticated company and arrived for lunch dressed accordingly.

Imagine their surprise when they met their American dining partners, each of whom was outfitted in a cotton T-shirt with the name of the new company emblazoned across it. Imagine their distaste when the Americans stretched across the table to hand the Frenchmen their own T-shirts, with the expectation that they would wear them at the meal.

The ensuing conversation did little to alleviate the discomfort. After pleasantries were exchanged, talk turned to the acquired company. Unfortunately, it quickly became apparent that the Americans had little understanding of the French business or its specific market. They had bought the company based purely on financial metrics. This may have made good mathematical sense, but it alienated the French. Little wonder then that the majority of the French executives present resigned from the company shortly thereafter.

The Americans in this story did not mean to be insulting. They just had not put the effort into preparing to "sell" to the French sensibility and suffered the negative costs and consequences as a result. As their experience illustrates, in any international setting, it is important to know exactly who you will be facing across the table.

DON'T RUSH THE RELATIONSHIP

A personal relationship is a proven aid to business transactions. While this is recognized in the networking activities most companies conduct in their established markets, many fail to invest the resources to network effectively in new markets. They can thus find themselves in a position of hurrying to make up for lost time once a prospective deal is on the table. Far better is a process of steady contact in locations of interest as part of the company's overall strategic planning program. This not only helps establish a basic framework of trust, but it can also reveal important insights into the other party's negotiating strategies and predilections, particularly when those parties would not normally have much else in common.

Finding the Common Ground

Diplomacy is easy when all parties like and trust each other. It is far harder to negotiate with someone whose views and basic ideology you disagree with. Still, whether or not you like your bargaining partners, the odds of getting what you need out of the deal improve when you can establish a common footing. Generally, this can only be done by investing time in the relationship. By seeking to understand the opposing point of view, as well as your deal-making partners' interests, objectives, and background, you can better define the window of opportunity that exists to satisfy your negotiating objective.

Bill Richardson, the former U.S. ambassador to the United Nations and current governor of New Mexico, is recognized around the world as a gifted diplomat. He was nominated for the Nobel Peace Prize four times, in 1995, 1997, 2000 and 2001. In his role as ambassador and international mediator, he has negotiated with a variety of regimes, from the Cubans to the Sudanese and the North Koreans, on issues ranging from the release of hostages to nuclear disarmament.

Time magazine in 1996 credited Richardson with "a knack for finding a warm spot in even the surliest of despots." In large part, this comes from Richardson's insistence on getting inside the mind of the opposing party. He does this both to understand that party's underlying motivation as well as, critically, to glean insight in establishing some form of common ground.

With respect to the North Koreans, for example, Richardson's investment in studying the relationship allowed him to discern the North Korean pattern of heightening a crisis as a negotiating ploy.[147] He was thus able to recognize the tactic for what it was and not allow it to distract attention from the more fundamental and shared concerns of the parties involved.

The ability to forge a common framework for discussion is essential to any successful and substantive conflict resolution. In all but the rarest of instances, acquiring this footing takes a substantial organizational investment in time and patience to cultivate. Don't rush. Give the relationship time to develop.

BUILD A TEAM

Teambuilding brings with it the sense of common purpose, a sense that is useful to cultivate even if team members come from opposing sides of the bargaining table. Veteran negotiators resort to teams or task forces as an aid to bring competing viewpoints together, sort out differences and, hopefully, arrive at a common ground. Specialists on a given topic, be it finance,

---

Teaming

You have to create the conditions and circumstances that will allow your business to be successful. Oftentimes, this involves not going it alone, but as a team.

---

integration or another domain, can hammer out technical details under the disciplining force of an assigned deadline.

Yet, the notion of team building has greater efficacy than the one-time resolution of a given deal or negotiation. It has applicability to the way successful companies establish themselves in foreign markets. With alliances and partnerships proliferating, business leaders must be every bit as concerned with their supply chain and alliance partners' needs and concerns as they are with their own.

A productive cross-border collaboration must be based on trust. Too often, in the haste to generate payback on an expensive overseas initiative, groups are pressured to deliver fast results. While understandable, this approach can undermine productivity. Team members, coming from different backgrounds either within the company or among multiple companies, have little time to learn what makes other members "tick," much less identify whether all have the same implicit project objectives and goals.

It is far easier to motivate high levels of commitment and productivity when participants have a vested interest in the outcome and care about the relationship. This is even more important in our knowledge-driven global economy. We're unlikely to divulge information with people we don't know. How do we know what the other person will do with the information? Will that individual reciprocate with other important knowledge? If not, will that tilt the power balance? Without a working framework built on trust, it can be extremely difficult to build and leverage inter-organizational relationships.

As communications expert Carol Kinsey Goman of Kinsey Consulting Services put it, "Taking time to build this 'social capital' at the beginning of a project increases the effectiveness of the team later on."[148] Goman adds, "Trust is fragile. Built slowly over time, it grows as people take small risks and wait for those acts of faith to be justified and reciprocated." [149] While building a network of productive, trusting relationships takes an investment of time, once that network is established it can greatly speed subsequent projects and transactions to completion. Parties are more able to "run with an idea" and just "get it done." Tapped in this manner, trusted relationships become a competitive asset.

BECOME VERSED IN CULTURAL DEAL-MAKING PREFERENCES

The world may be getting more connected and business seeping across borders, but entrenched cultural issues remain. Understanding these nuances is as important as understanding the specific business terms of a proposed deal under negotiation. Cross-cultural sensitivity is essential to developing the political astuteness to remain innovative and responsive to shifting competitive and global developments.

Without putting too fine a point on cultural generalities, western business executives may prefer to cut quickly to the point while Asian executives often prefer a more deliberative approach. Japanese and Chinese business people are generally more reluctant to divulge information early in the negotiation, whereas European and Americans are often more open to imparting key information in order to advance contract discussions. British and American companies appreciate PowerPoint graphics, charts and boards articulating the message. European and Asian counterparts can sometimes view such presentations as insufficient, preferring detailed discussion of numbers and financial metrics to speeches and slides.

But while it is instructive to reach for one's "Doing Business in . . ." guide to refresh on cultural nuances, that alone will not succeed in getting you much past the epidermis. Breaking through to the mind of your international counterpart requires leveraging an awareness of cultural differences and building from there.

What's the Objective?

Different cultures can have different negotiating goals. Some may go into a negotiation with a goal of walking out with a contract. Others see their objective as coming away with a relationship. Not recognizing the other side's expectations can lead to major problems.

For instance, it is useful to know that in some cultures the first few rounds of business meetings are not typically expected to ink a deal, but rather to kick the tires of the forming relationship, observes Professor Jeswald Salacuse of Tufts University's Fletcher School of Diplomacy. In other first meetings, he notes it is hoped one might emerge with a contract or, at the very least, agreement on terms for a second round of meetings.

Whatever the specific objective, it is important that at least one side articulates it. That way, one's briskness, for example, may be understood as a means to an end and not as an attempt to avoid engaging the other side in a thorough discussion of the details. Your negotiating partners may still push back at the pace, but at least they will understand the underlying motivation for what it is and not misconstrue it in a potentially harmful manner.

Such was Enron's unwitting experience in India. Back in the mid-1990s, before the energy company had mushroomed into the fatally-flawed conglomerate it became, Enron attempted to negotiate a long-term electricity supply contract between its Indian subsidiary, Dabhol Power, and the Maharashtra state government. As Rebecca Mark, then chairman and CEO of Enron International stated in *BusinessWeek*, "We were extremely concerned with time, because time is money for us."[150]

By pursuing the deal quickly and aggressively, however, Enron raised the back and suspicions of the Indian public who assumed the government was not protecting their interests properly. Responding to their outrage, the Indian government eventually cancelled the deal, concluding that negotiations were conducted in "unseemly haste."[151] It took Enron five years, 24 lawsuits and approvals from three successive Indian governments to finally reverse the cancellation. Time is money. Don't waste it by assuming that your counterparts feel the same way about it as you do.

Understanding each party's objective is one thing. Determining what approach to use is another. Should the tack be a problem-solving one or is a no-concessions approach better? Negotiating experts tussle over whether it is smarter to approach a cross-border discussion with a "win-win" strategy or not. Some argue that in trying to deliver a solution that all parties feel good about can instead result in a diluted solution that aids no one particularly well. Others suggest that the quality of the relationship is paramount, even if compromise is required to keep it on firm footing. The right answer must be dictated by organizational priorities and an analysis of the potential risks and rewards at stake. Either way, a strategic deliberation of the appropriate negotiating approach must accompany the upfront assessment of your side's objective.

UNDERSTAND THE NATURE AND LIKELIHOOD OF GOVERNMENT INTERVENTION

Political acuity is another important dimension of commercial diplomacy. In August 2005, the China National Offshore Oil Corp. (CNOOC) dropped its US$18.5 billion takeover bid for the U.S. based Unocal company. CNOOC, which is predominantly controlled by the Chinese government, left the heated takeover battle because of what they called, "the political environment in the U.S." They were referring to the active intervention of the U.S. Congress and others who opposed the deal fearing foreign control of a key energy enterprise. The story is more than just a deal gone sour. In a way it reveals a certain "coming-of-age" lesson for an extraordinarily talented set of Chinese business leaders still getting accustomed to the mores of global capitalism.

In recent years, China has sought to acquire western brand names to bootstrap powerful, but less-well-known Chinese businesses to a global presence. In 2004, Chinese computer manufacturer Lenovo acquired IBM's personal computer business. In the summer of 2005, Nanjing Automobile acquired the British flagship automaker MG Rover. Still, China's global march has had its bumps, of which the failed Unocal purchase is perhaps the most emblematic. As Paul Maidment observed in *Forbes*, "China's national interest is its imperative, and cross-border M&A is the way to fulfill it . . . But they will have to learn how to win at this most capitalist of games, M&A."[152]

As Chinese businesses gain important battle lessons from their takeover experience in the West, so too must their American and continental peers learn the ways of the East. "Government intervention [in China] makes my life very difficult," responded Anthony C. Hooper, president of Bristol-Myers Squibb Intercontinental Region, in a Harvard Business School panel, recalling how last-minute pricing interference by the Chinese government whipped the cloth from under the carefully prepared set of financial documents he had just completed.[153]

Indeed, today there remains considerable confusion among foreign businesses over the best ways to work with the Chinese government. In part, this stems from the dual role between a Chinese entity's regulators and shareholders. Often as not, they are one and the same. Navigating whom to turn to for what can be confusing. Successful entrants in the Chinese marketplace generally recommend engaging a local, China-based law firm to assist. Mark Newman, vice president and CFO for GM Shanghai, remarked at the same Harvard round-table that, "It's important to have a good joint venture partner to help negotiate the bureaucracy and influence government policy with your interests in mind . . . so that negotiations can focus on implementing, not defining, the company's mission."[154]

Understanding these best practices is part of the journey. Replicating them across a global footprint can be enervating. The Chinese market, with its command economy underpinnings, brings with it a particular set of complexities, but all nations have political "hot buttons" that foreign entrants must endeavor to understand if they wish to avoid costly missteps.

When rumors swirled that the U.S. company PepsiCo was preparing a takeover bid for the French company Danone, it was enough to make French President Jacques Chirac halt his trip to Madagascar and return to France. The rumored bid hit a national nerve. The French daily paper *Le Figaro* ran a report calling PepsiCo an "American ogre."[155] French politicians termed Danone a "national jewel" and vowed to do whatever it takes to block an American takeover. The reaction led PepsiCo to issue an announcement stating it was not pursuing a takeover bid for the French yogurt maker. This forced denial came following the news that the company had already acquired 3% of Danone's stock, which they may now need to unwind at what may possibly be a less favorable price.

While estimating how deep public and political sentiment runs over a specific national company or resource involves a certain degree of educated guesswork, it requires fewer guesses and basic due diligence to test the waters in advance. Indeed, it is possible that the rumors of the Danone takeover were PepsiCo's trial balloon, the noise of whose pop quickly told the company what it needed to know about whether to invest the time and resources in proceeding further.

The more one is embedded in a given location, the more options one has for reaching into established networks to gauge political sensitivities and the extent of possible government intervention. In those cases where one has no direct presence, the engagement of a respected and established intermediary can provide appropriate insight and experience.

ETHICAL CONSIDERATIONS

Professional conduct and integrity are mainstays in guiding the health and character of a business. But what to do when operating in fractious international settings where the rule of law is thinly applied and the judiciary weak?

Bribery and corruption are virtually accepted modes of business in certain parts of the world. This places foreign enterprises with more evolved governance structures in a bit of a quandary. If one participates in this unsavory form of business, one reduces the company's standards and risks sullying its name and reputation. If one does not participate, one must stand idly by as less conscience-bound competitors rake in all the business.

The Organization for Economic Cooperation and Development (OECD) and a consortium of nations around the world have all issued formal anti-corruption standards that make participation in such schemes a crime. Still, *CFO.com* reports that Germany's "Corruption Perceptions Index," based on bribery data and surveys performed by the NGO Transparency International, found "rampant corruption" in 60 countries.[156] The report suggests that the price paid by companies that retain the ethical high ground, has been steep. The U.S. State Department acknowledges significant allegations of bribery by foreign firms from 1994 to 2001, involving over 400 contracts around the world and US$200 billion.

During the Africa Economic Summit of the World Economic Forum in June 2005, Klaus Döring, Deputy Chairman of Siemens in South Africa, showed the increasingly firm response some multinationals are taking in response to the worldwide corruption issue. He mentioned that Siemens employs a global chief compliance officer charged with enforcing worldwide adherence to company ethics standards. Managers are required to sign Siemens' anti-corruption code. If they do not, they are prohibited from doing business with the company. Döring remarked, "We lose some contracts, but very few."[157] Other companies, such as Unilever, Motorola, and Microsoft, employ a similarly tough stance, requiring employees, vendors and suppliers to sign anti-bribery and anti-corruption contracts.

Ultimately, an open society with a free press, active NGOs, and financial accountability and transparency are the best devices for curbing corruption. The best companies are tying anti-corruption standards to their global compliance programs and require full reporting and disclosure from all international affiliates. Effective auditing and internal control guidelines will remain critical in providing the detailed oversight to reduce ethical malfeasance. As the world's dominant economies and their leading companies come together, effective commercial diplomacy must demonstrate a zero-tolerance stance against corruption in both principles and practice.

CONCLUSION

Modern business negotiations involve a tangle of influential constituencies. Failure to connect productively with one's commercial partners can jeopardize the best-laid plans and the most promising deals.

Sophisticated global businesses understand the diplomatic dimensions of their leadership role. As with political diplomacy, sincerity, transparency and honesty go a long way toward building trust. This is aided through patient investment in long-term relationships, exhaustive preparation, teaming and recognition of cultural sensitivities and negotiating styles.

Diplomacy is an art, perhaps the quintessential expression of what some term "people skills." As such, it is informed by alternative perspectives, ideologies, communication and expression. The most experienced commercial diplomats reflect this richness. It is what allows them to negotiate from a position of strength and to demonstrate grace in responding to conflict. Its embodiment forms a key underpinning of successful global leaders.

CHAPTER 10

Leadership

"There is great force hidden in gentle command."
—George Herbert, seventeenth-century poet

Today's leaders must assume the mantle of a broader leadership role to address the impact of globalization, maximize profitability, and advance the interests of their company, their employees and their stakeholders. In light of these dynamics, multinational CEOs face a leadership brief that consists of the following precepts:

❏ To deliver on their organizational potential, they must create an integrated value map in which they identify core strengths, tie these to core strategy, and embed the resulting direction in their process flow.

❏ To be responsive, they must change from the outside-in, studying their customers, watching their competitors and leading their industry. They will develop an organization that is self-sufficient and fast, suited to capturing and responding to competitive intelligence.

❑ To deliver with excellence, they must create a performance meritocracy, one that offers a rewarding, attractive and challenging work environment.

❑ To execute with speed, they must remove internal boundaries and foster an environment that allows innovation to flourish, whether vertically, from the bottom of the organization up, or horizontally, through acquisition.

❑ To endure, they must know their markets and reflect the impact of local market sensitivities, challenging facts and conventional wisdom, but never losing sight of the principles and ethics upon which the business was founded.

All of this requires extraordinary leadership. We conclude this book by examining the qualities of leadership most in demand on our global stage and what companies are doing to develop the next generation of corporate leaders.

LEADERS GROOMING LEADERS

Great leaders know how to lead other leaders. Jim Owens, Caterpillar's CEO, is a case in point. A PhD economist, Owens has worked in Europe, Asia and in the American heartland throughout his 33-year career with the company. In that time, he has served as corporate economist and held numerous management positions in accounting, product source planning, operations and finance. Indeed, there is not much Owens hasn't touched or overseen at Caterpillar, nor grappled with in forecasting the health of its business and markets. It is a combination that might lead to hubris in some. Not so with Owens, whose low-key leadership style is notable for its openness in soliciting the input of others.

Many executives might quaver at the thought of openly challenging their leader's plans for fear of possible recriminations. Yet, Owens embraces constructive discourse from his senior staff. In fact, he demands it. At the company's Peoria, Illinois headquarters, strategic planning sessions are marked by spirited discussion and active questioning by all participants. Caterpillar's Dave Burritt admits the environment surprised him when he first became CFO. "I've never seen anybody invite criticism the way that Jim does," he says.[158] "He lets people exhaust themselves. We'll challenge something or say 'this doesn't make any sense.' And he'll listen and incorporate the thoughts of others into the framework. He is just an outstanding leader."[159]

Looking back, Burritt laughs, reflecting that in other environments many of his impassioned criticisms would get someone like him fired. The fact that the heavy equipment manufacturer welcomes such thoughtful input is something Burritt finds both enabling and emboldening. He speaks with genuine passion for his work at Caterpillar—the company is one of the original, continuous members of the first Fortune 500 list—and is clearly eager to effect meaningful change in sustaining Caterpillar's long history of success.

By making it okay for leadership to ask thoughtful questions, challenge conventional wisdom and consider alternative strategies, leaders like Caterpillar's Jim Owens empower management and employees to think, to test, and ultimately to refine their forward direction. Moreover, they demonstrate that great leaders are both stewards and guides.

REDUCE RISK BY CULTIVATING GLOBAL TALENT

Every entity has its own risk appetite, one that ties to the company's culture, industry and strategy. Americans, for example, are generally regarded as risk takers, Asian cultures less so, and Europeans somewhere in the middle. Benoit Potier, chairman of the French company Air Liquide, interviewed in *Chief Executive* magazine, emphasized this stating that "risk-taking is culture specific. That's why we need diversity in management."[160] He suggests that rotations and other personnel assignments can help develop that diversity.

> *Global Opportunity*
> Risk sensitivity can vary by culture. As multinationals expand, the global face regional managers exhibit can determine a company's ability to spot and seize appropriate opportunities.

The ability to map professional competencies to global roles, the likes of which the rigors of international competitiveness demand, goes hand-in-hand with the development of a strong and strongly dispersed global management bench. As part of Matsushita's "Leap Ahead 21" plan for instance, the company seeks to derive 60% of its overall profits from its overseas operations. As their balance of trade shifts, Matsushita is learning several things about itself. For instance, Matsushita president, Kunio Nakamura, noted, "In the past, we tried to manage with our own human resources under the conviction that the Matsushita way of management should only be led by Japanese."[161] He and the company have since changed that perception and are now, as Nakamura stresses, "replacing Japanese management with locally hired management." He adds that the company has also initiated a specialized training program for local resources in various geographies in order to help groom them for the higher management ranks.

GLOBAL ASSIGNMENTS ARE CRITICAL

Dan O'Bryant is CFO for the Fortune 500 company Avery Dennison and a fervent believer in the importance of gaining first-hand international experience. In an interview for his business school alma mater, the University of Southern California, he observed, "You find that business is a lot more complex overseas. You introduce cultures, currencies and a new set of regulations. All of those things go into managing the company, so you really lack something if you haven't had that experience."[162]

Passport to Leadership

"If you're working at a multinational and you haven't been out of the U.S., you're really handicapped in your ability to be in a management role." *Daniel O'Bryant, CFO, Avery Dennison*

He notes specifically that an aspiring finance professional requires a thorough knowledge of the multitude of international financial regulations. In addition, one must learn how to manage and mitigate currency fluctuation and transfer pricing risks, issues important to anyone wishing to advance to a position of senior finance leadership. Yet, a manager whose duties were strictly domestic-bound would be unlikely to have much exposure to those subjects.

Exposure to different experiences, cultures, work styles and personalities allows managers to adapt and respond to changing situations. As they grow in their careers, international assignments are an important means of giving prospective leaders the opportunity to develop the support of global stakeholders, partners and customers, as well as acquire needed experience implementing the set of decisions upon which the success of their projects depends.

IN SEARCH OF GLOBAL TALENT

A study by Karl Moore, a professor at McGill University in Canada and Associate Fellow of Templeton College at Oxford University, finds that certain countries seem to have a particular ability to turn out high-quality global managers.[163] After more than 10 years of research with leading companies such as Hewlett-Packard, Nokia, Pfizer, IBM and others, Moore identified 10 nations as generating an above average cluster of superior global leaders: Canada, Switzerland, Belgium, Singapore, Norway, Sweden, the Netherlands, Denmark, Australia and Finland.

Puzzling over why this should be, Moore concludes that all 10 countries occupy an economic rung just below that of the world's largest military and economic powers. This means, they tend to pay close attention to the personality and positioning of other countries around them, economically, politically and culturally.

Canadians, for example, living beside the sprawling power of the United States, can't help but be affected by the flow of American culture washing over their border. The same can be said of such Northern European countries as Belgium and the Netherlands, surrounded by a host of cultural influences from their European Community neighbors. In these diverse local environments, multi-cultural sensitivity is not so much adopted as absorbed. Isolationism is not an option.

Translated to business, Moore suggests that, "From a marketing point of view, empathizing with your customer's culture is paramount. Finns and Canadians do this naturally, not because they are better people but because it comes to them naturally as citizens of a multicultural environment."[164]

These findings are interesting. Far from dashing the hopes of CEO aspirants in other countries, they simply underscore the value of a global-centric experience in helping managers lead and respond to the needs of international markets.

TONE AT THE TOP

Sony set an institutional precedent for itself in 2005 by appointing Howard Stringer its first foreign-born CEO. That same year, Royal Dutch Shell appointed outgoing Nokia CEO and Finn, Jorma Ollila, to serve as its non-executive chairman. A couple of years earlier, Indian-born Arun Sarin replaced Sir Christopher Gent as head of British telecommunications giant Vodafone. And, Carlo Gutierrez, a Cuban-born US citizen, was elevated from his post as head of the Kellogg Company to serve as U.S. Commerce Secretary at the request of President George Bush. Over the years, other multinational companies have taken the similar step of appointing a non-national to the top office.

Among other skills, these non-native CEOs and chairmen bring a new focus and cultural sophistication that can jog perspective and change traditional behaviors. Instead of tolerance for old precepts such as "this is the way we've always done it," a company may be inclined to try something more innovative. The objectivity such a leader can provide may also help in cataloging organizational strengths, weaknesses and opportunities. Their international perspective can globalize the company's external face and brand as well, bringing an international sensitivity to customer relationships.

One reason foreign-born CEOs are effective for U.S. companies, writes Dale Buss of *Chief Executive* magazine, "is that they understand in a more visceral, firsthand way than American-born counterparts that their companies must let go of the notion that international operations are simply extensions of the U.S.-focused strategy."[165] If you have lived and worked in one location most of your career, you may not be able to see the same opportunities.

Simply put, to succeed in today's global economy one must have a personal connection to the world beyond one's own borders.

IDENTIFYING TOMORROW'S GLOBAL LEADERS

The strongest companies take pains to track high-potential talent, not just to carry out their corporate mission and objectives, but also to plan for succession. Some companies have appointed rising stars to the CEO position only to find their range of experience was too narrow for the broad demands of a global executive. An individual who may have risen through the marketing ranks and had tremendous success launching and managing global product lines may falter when it comes to the operational and financial experience needed to talk the language of Wall Street effectively—providing an unpleasant reality check for both the company and the employee.

The global HR consultancy Hewitt performed a study of 100 multinational companies. Their research revealed that each of the best-performing companies, those occupying the top quartile in terms of total shareholder return, had formal methodologies for identifying and developing star performers.[166] That cluster of 25 companies stood apart for their active involvement in charting challenging, attractive and individualized career maps for their upcoming leadership group, something that was uniquely true of the top echelon companies and was far more uneven in the lower tiers.

While succession planning and leadership development are time-intensive, few would dispute the linkage between effective management training and strong bottom line returns.

TASTING SUCCESS—NESTLÉ

"Leadership development is perhaps one of the most important duties I have," says Peter Brabeck-Letmathe, CEO of Swiss-based Nestlé. Largely because of its strength in recognizing, training and developing a worldwide bench of global talent, Nestlé took the number one spot in *Chief Executive Magazine*'s annual ranking of the "Best Companies for Leaders."[167] Indeed, Nestlé has always been vocal about its commitment to its people, a commitment proclaimed in company literature and even more demonstrably in their executive training camps.

Each year, Nestlé selects 2,000 young executives from its offices and facilities throughout the world to enter their elite leadership training program held at the food conglomerate's executive development center in Vevey, Switzerland. There, the candidates spend a full month interacting with senior Nestlé leadership, working with global peers, and attending specialized training on Nestlé's vision, strategy and goals.[168]

In 2004, Nestlé delivered 18.7% net income growth. Today, it stands as the number one food company by sales in the world. Without doubt, the company's base of highly-trained international leaders is one factor behind its success.

"YOU CAN DO IT. WE CAN HELP."—
HOME DEPOT

Bob Nardelli, CEO of Home Depot, came to the "Do It Yourself" leader from GE and is trying to infuse some of the same human resources discipline at his new company. Profiled in *Fortune*, Nardelli began his own career as a manufacturing engineer for GE before working his way through the ranks. Having been in the proverbial trenches, he recognizes how critical it is for world-class companies to take an active role in coaching future leaders.

Indeed, Nardelli is more active than many CEOs in bringing a disciplined, long-term mindset to succession planning. Noel Tichy, a management professor at the University of Michigan Business School, and former director of GE's Crotonville center, was quoted in the *Fortune* article, stating, "They are building the most systematic teaching organization that I've seen in a retailer."[169]

In addition to overseeing the building of a new executive development center near Home Depot's headquarters in Atlanta, Nardelli participates actively in each of his officers' performance reviews, taking copious notes and personally reviewing every promotion. Why does he take such unusual care? "I absolutely believe that people, unless coached, never reach their maximum capabilities," Nardelli says.[170] He is adamant that the ability to create a coaching environment, one that permeates the entire enterprise, is a critical differentiator in selecting, nurturing, preparing and retaining future leaders.

As companies refine their approach toward grooming the right global talent, they will look to offer key employees the opportunity to:

❑ Engage in an international secondment.

❑ Supervise a cross-border project.

❑ Lead a multinational product or project team.

❑ Lead a foreign-based or global client account.

These experiences help aspiring managers acquire a track record in important leadership areas. They provide exposure to the requirements of pulling together, coaching and managing cross-border teams, and contact with diverse cultural and political sensitivities, skills they will need as they execute their organization's strategic priorities.

MAPPING COMPETENCIES— CASCADING KNOWLEDGE

BMW CFO Stefan Krause told us that "An attractive working environment is like a mosaic made up of many pieces of different sizes."[171] We couldn't agree more.

At the BMW Group, the mosaic's components include clearly-defined agreements on targets for employees, a cooperative style of management, a wide range of further education and training programs, and flexible work time models designed to strike a balance between professional and private life.

Given the importance of skilled-knowledge workers in the global knowledge economy, consultants, practitioners and business leaders are starting to lay out their own development mosaics, injecting science into the art of mapping an organization's skills competencies. Among the most needed are strategic thinking, the ability to create productive client relationships, creativity, team building, intellectual strength, motivation and personality. Armed with these and a set of defined performance expectations, the organization is more or less ready to begin inventorying its knowledge base.

Deployed across an enterprise, these measures can provide a consistent basis for determining where a company sits with respect to a needed skill, whether they are heavy in one area, such as strong client relationships or lighter in another, such as innovative thinking. Such insight can strengthen the company's ability to correct gaps—either by rotating, hiring or training staff. It also provides the opportunity to establish more tailored career enrichment to round out an employee's knowledge set.

The global pharmaceutical company Eli Lilly is a leader in using competency mapping to identify and develop key staff, a process they call the Group Development Review (GDR). Management author Jay Conger highlights the company for instilling what he calls "learning in action." In his report for the *Harvard Business Review*, he mentions that Lilly's GDR program is compulsory for the roughly 500 or so professionals identified by Lilly's talent assessment program. As Conger and article co-author, Robert Fulmer, detail:

> "The GDR is a periodic, in-depth review of a single person, involving input from both past and present supervisors

(the employee is not present for the meeting). In a facilitated ninety-minute discussion, the group identifies the next steps the employee should take, gathering input from others in the organization, if necessary."[172]

> ### Leveraging Learning at the World Bank
>
> Few organizations need to leverage global resources with as much dexterity as the World Bank. *Chief Learning Officer Magazine* reports that "To strengthen the strategic focus of the World Bank's learning efforts, its strategic learning centers and regions use professional and technical learning road maps to articulate how learning activities support business objectives." The bank views these learning road maps as a critical success factor in enabling them to cascade global knowledge. *Chief Learning Officer Magazine, March 2005*

The employee's supervisor presents the results of the discussion to the individual and works with him or her in tailoring an appropriately directed career plan. For instance, if the process reveals that a given professional has strong team-building skills but little overseas experience, plans might be made to offer the employee a suitable international rotation of the sort necessary for top-level advancement.

Far from simply a head office operation, Eli Lilly has unrolled its talent development program throughout its worldwide enterprise. Rajiv Gulati, Chairman of Eli Lilly India, for one, is passionate about the benefits this disciplined approach to training and development brings to his unit.

Interviewed for India's management magazine *The Smart Manager*, Gulati describes how they use two best practices— an employee-focused Potential Assessment Committee (PAC) and an advancement-focused Talent Assessment Committee (TAC)—to assess his organization's skills base.

The PAC assesses an individual's performance history along with his or her ability to learn and assimilate new information quickly. The TAC examines the person's current skill level and compares that to the skills required of the next rung in their career progression. Together, they provide the company with insight into how best to enhance the employee's capabilities. These insights are then folded into a personalized career-development plan.

This knowledge helps Lilly develop a keen understanding of its surfeits and shortages of talent. For proof of its success, Gulati points to its lowered attrition rates, the fact that the affiliate regularly tops India's "Best Places to Work" lists, and the unit's own growth, which as of 2003, outpaced its industry group by a margin of three-to-one.

Indeed, with people today serving as the most important asset for many global competitors, it stands to reason that those companies that excel at defining, inventorying and developing their strongest talent will be in the strongest position to compete.

FROM CULTIVATING THE MIND OF THE LEADER TO REVEALING THE SOUL

The advent of free markets, the increase in economic liberalization and the spread of technology are propelling the march of globalization, weaving together formerly separate disciplines. This puts unprecedented opportunities in reach for smart, agile businesses, and unprecedented demands in front of those seeking to lead them.

In response, CEOs and managers require fluency across many dimensions, not all of them part of the traditional slate of management responsibilities. They must demonstrate the character, wisdom and motivational qualities associated with diplomats and statesmen, as well as the business acumen expected of senior corporate leadership. They must also, more than ever, be able to leverage the institutional capacity of their organizations, maximizing the productivity and return on all of their assets.

The blending of businessperson and commercial diplomat is just one output of the layered dimensions of our entangled world economy. The advancement of prosperity, particularly in the most economically ravaged parts of the world, is tied to increased political stability and business opportunity. Businesses that champion integrity recognize the imperative to groom talent of similar character, professionals who will stand up for appropriate engagement in corporate social responsibility.

In an address to Stanford University, Bill George, former chairman and CEO of Medtronic and author of *Authentic Leadership*, called for a new and modern leader, "one who checks his ego at the door and maintains an attitude of serving others."[173] He said the most powerful leaders will have what he calls "heart qualities," an ability to stay true to one's core values despite the inevitable distractions of business life, adding, "If you do that well, you'll have people following you to the ends of the earth, buying your products and services, and investing in your company." To cultivate this, George feels strongly that leadership development programs must nurture not only important business fundamentals, but critical people skills as well. "The easiest part of any job is working the numbers." Far harder, he said, "is bringing a group of people together and motivating them toward a common goal with a consistent set of values."

In many respects this gets to the soft but powerful driving force of leadership, its ability to inspire. People want to be rewarded for good work, but equally they want to believe their work contributes to the greater good—wherein the benefits of corporate growth are broadly shared, and in which globalization means rising incomes and opportunities for a wider swath of the world's population.

CONCLUSION

This book was written to help business men and women build companies designed to win in our global economy. As we have seen, there are many requirements, from unified marketing to integrated operations, from compliance with today's financial and regulatory needs, to imagining the strategic decisions we'll need to make 20 years from now.

Distilled to a short list, to be designed to win you must identify what it is you stand for and where it is you are going; you must isolate your key assets and bring them together—

human, technological and otherwise; you must listen to understand and reflect your understanding in the way you communicate; you must show your customers that you are willing to take risks for their benefit, while demonstrating to your stakeholders how well those risks are being managed with integrity. You must take responsibility not only for your own performance and that of your company, but also for the weight of your own leadership, recognizing that those to whom much has been given, much is expected. You must lead with sensitivity, a soft characteristic in a relatively hard-nosed world, but one that allows companies to build trusted relationships across borders that advance and sustain the interests of all involved. Above all, you must recognize that success is best nurtured and accomplished because of the efforts of your people.

Bibliography

http://www.aaaa.org/transcripts/transcripts.html.

Aron, Ravi, Remarks before the 2005 World Economic Forum, Davos Switzerland.

"Best Workplaces 2005," *Financial Times*, April 27, 2005.

Bialik, Carl, "Measuring the Impact of Blogs Requires More Than Just Counting," *The Wall Street Journal Online*, May 26, 2005.

Boyer, Nicole, "Reperceiving Business From the Bottom Up." Global Business Network, *GBN Working Paper*, 2003.

Boyes, William, *The New Managerial Economics*, Chapter Ten, "The Firm's Architecture: Organization and Corporate Culture," Houghton Mifflin, 2003.

Bradford, Roslyn, "Management Across Borders, *Alumni Profiles*, University of Southern California.

Breen, Bill, "Living in Dell Time," *Fast Company*, November, 2004, Issue 88.

Business Innovation Consortium, http://www.bicnow.com/what/EVPPOV.pdf.

Business Today, August 7–21, 2000.

"You have to be Pushy and Aggressive," *BusinessWeek*, February 24, 1997. http://bwnt.businessweek.com/brand/2005/.

Buss, Dale, "Non-American CEOs are having a big impact at traditional U.S. companies," *Chief Executive*, April 2004.

Buss, Dale, "Little Giants: You don't have to be big to be global," *Chief Executive*, May 2004.

Canon, Michael, Remarks before the 2005 World Economic Forum, Davos, Switzerland.

Cappelli, Peter, "The Futility of Golden Handcuffs," *Harvard Business Review*, Jan/Feb 2000, Vol 78.

Carlotti Jr., Stephen J, Mary Ellen Coe and Jesko Perrey, "Making Brand Portfolios Work," The McKinsey Quarterly, 2004, Number 4.

Chanda, Nayan, "What Is Globalization," Yale Center for the Study of Globalization, http://www.ycsg.yale.edu/center/index.html and http://yaleglobal.yale.edu/about/.

Charan, Ram, "Managing to Be Best." *Time Magazine*, http://www.time.com/time/time100/builder/other/managers.html

Colyer, Edwin, "Prescribing a Global Identity," Brandchannel.com.

"The Compliance Journey: Balancing Risk and Controls with Business Improvement," KPMG LLP, 2004.

Conger, Jay and Robert Fulmer, "Bench Strength: Grooming Your Next CEO," *Harvard Business School Working Knowledge*, January 19, 2004. Based on an excerpt from "Developing Your Leadership Pipeline," *Harvard Business Review*, December 2003.

Court, David, Jonathan Gordon and Jesko Perrey, "Boosting Returns on Marketing Investment," *The McKinsey Quarterly*, 2005, No 2.

"Corruption: Cutting the Cost of Doing Business," Africa Economic Summit, World Economic Forum, January 6, 2005.

Craumer, Martha, "How to Think Strategically About Outsourcing," *Harvard Management Update*, Vol. 7, No. 5, May 2002.

Daum, Juergen, H., "How Scenario Planning Can Significantly Reduce Strategic Risks and Boost Value in the Innovation Chain." The New Economist Analyst Report, September 8, 2001.

Dawson, Chester, *Lexus: The Relentless Pursuit*, John Wiley & Sons, 2004.

De Capele, Gaetan, "Une ligne de defense très politique," *Le Figaro*, July 20, 2005.

DePalma, Donald, "The First of Three P's for Global Marketing," *CMO*, May, 2005.

"The Development Gateway Special Report: Foreign Investment and Development—Who Gains?" Development Gateway, February 21, 2005.

"Development and Globalization: Facts and Figures 2004," *Trade and Development Report 2002*, UNCTAD.

Dorf, Paul R., Compensation Resources, Inc., Press Release, Sept, 2004.

EBS, "Offshore Outsourcing Basics," http://www.ebstrategy.com/outsourcing/basics/definition.htm.

The Economist,
"The Ethics of Business," January 20′ 2005.
"Profit and the Public Good," January 20, 2005.
"The World According to CSR," January 20, 2005.

Engardio, Peter and Dexter Roberts, "The China Price," *Business-Week*, December 6, 2004.

Flexible Employment Optios (FEO), "The Business Case for Flexible Working Conditions," Project Summary, November 2004.

Flynn, Tim and McCarthy, Mary Pat, *Risk: From the CEO and Board Perspective*, McGraw-Hill, 2003.

Fuld, Leonard, "Business Tsunamis are Approaching. Learn How to Prepare," *Pharmaceutical Executive*, May 1, 2004.

George, Bill, "Becoming a leader of heart and soul," Address to Stanford University's Graduate School of Business, April 2004.

"Global Footprint Design—Mastering the Rules of International Value Creation," Study, June 2004.

Goodall, Keith and Burgers, Willem, "Frequent Fliers" China Business Review, March 1998.

Gottlieb, Scott, "Big Pharma Goes Shopping: Who's Next?" *Forbes*, June 16, 2005.

Groundwater, Fergus, "The Branham Leadership Series: Management Strategies for Success in IT's Turbulent Times," and Zook, Chris and Rigby, Darrell, "How to Think Strategically in a Recession," *Harvard Management Update*, November 2001.

Hafrey, Leigh, "Proseminar on Narrative, Ethics, and Teaching in the Workplace." Also Shaw, Gordon and Brown, Robert, "Strategic Stories: How 3M is Rewriting Business Planning," *Harvard Business Review*, May–June 1998.

Hagel, John III, "Offshoring goes on the offensive," The McKinsey Quarterly, 2004, Number 2.

Hamm, Steve, "IBM: More than Emergency Surgery," Business-Week Online, May 5, 2005.

Hammonds, Keith H. "Size is Not a Strategy," *Fast Company*, September 2002, Issue 62.

Hanna, Julia, "MNCs in Asia: Investing in the Future," *HBS Bulletin*, February 25, 2002.

Hemerling, Jeff and Dave Young, "Navigating the Five Currents of Globalization: How Leading Companies Are Capturing Global Advantage," Boston Consulting Group, January 2005.

"Building High-Potential Leaders." Study, Hewitt, http://was4.hewitt.com/hewitt/resource/articleindex/talent/grooming.htm.

Hoblitzell, Tom, "CEO Perspectives: Business Planning in Inclement Economic Weather," *DM Review Magazine*, June, 2002.

Home Depot, http://www.homedepot.com/HDUS/EN_US/corporate/about/eoc.shtml.

Hornblower, Sam, "Wal-Mart & China: A Joint Venture," supplement to the documentary "Is Wal-Mart Good for America?" by Frontline for WGBH Public Broadcasting, November 23, 2004.

HR Magazine, April 1996.

Huyett, William and Patrick Viguerie, "Extreme Competition," *The McKinsey Quarterly*, January 26, 2005.

Hyndai.co.in, Press release, "Hyundai achieves 105% domestic growth in April-May period," June 2005.

http://www.ibm.com/news/us/en/2005/01/patents.html.

Iritani, Evelyn and Dickerson, Marla, "Tallying Port Dispute's Costs," *Los Angeles Times*, November 25, 2002.

Jain, Kuldeep, Nigel Manson and Shirish Sankhe, "The right passage to India," The McKinsey Quarterly, February 2005.

Jewkes, John, David Sawers and Richard Stillerman, *The Sources of Invention*, 1958; 2nd ed., 1969.

Katz, David, "The Bribery Gap," CFO.com, January 1, 2005.

Kinsey Goman, Carol, "Five reasons people don't tell what they know," Knowledge Management, June 2, 2002 http://www.kmmag.com/articles/default.asp?ArticleID=960.

Kirkpatrick, David; Roth, Daniel, "10 Tech Trends: Why There's No Escaping the Blog," *Fortune Magazine*, December 27, 2004.

Kleiner, Art, "The Man Who Saw the Future," *Strategy + Business*, Spring 2003.

Knuchel, Francois, "CAMI Technology Transfer Project," Synergy Associates.

Kothar, S.P.; Libert, Barry, "Value of Investment in Intangibles," *MIT Sloan Management Review*, Fall 2001, Vol. 43, No. 1.

KPMG International
  Interview with Stefan Krause, CFO, BMW Group, August 2, 2005
  Interview with Kunio Nakamura, President, Matsushita Electric Industrial Co., Ltd, August 22, 2005.
  Interview with Jim Owens and Dave Burritt, CEO and CFO of Caterpillar Inc., July 18, 2005.
  Interview with Arvind Sodhani, President, Intel Capital, July 22, 2005.

Interview with Katsuaki Watanabe, President, Toyota Motor Corporation, October 19, 2005.

"The Compliance Journey: Balancing Risk and Controls with Business Improvement," 2004.

"The Compliance Journey: Making Compliance Sustainable," 2005.

"Tax in the Boardroom: A Discussion Paper," 2004.

KPMG LLP (UK)

*"Intellectual Gold,"*2002.

KPMG LLP (US)

"M&A Forum Highlights" March 2005.

Lagace, Martha, "How to Put Meaning Back into Leading," *HBS Working Knowledge*, HBSWK Interview with Joel M. Podolny, Rakesh Khurana, and Marya Hill-Popper, Pub. Date: Jan 10, 2005.

Lee, Hau L., "The Triple-A Supply Chain," *Harvard Business Review*, Vol. 82, No. 10, October 2004.

Lev, Baruch, "Remarks on the Measurement, Valuation and Reporting of Intangible Assets," Federal Reserve Bank of New York Policy Review, September 2003.

Liss, David, "Bill Richardson: 'Find the Common Thread,'" BusinessWeek online, November 13, 2003.

Maidment, Paul, "Washington Politics Shock Chinese," *Forbes*, August 2, 2005.

Mann, Catherine L., "Globalization of IT Services and White Collar Jobs: The Next Wave of Productivity Growth" International Economics Policy Briefs, Number PB03-11, December 2003.

Manzella, John, "Globalization's Effects," A World Connected, aworldconnected.org, September 1, 2002.

Melvin, Sheila, Special Report: Human Resources, "Retaining Chinese Employees," *China Business Review*, November-December 2001.

Mehta, Sankar, "GE's outsourcing departure sets a new trend—outsource headaches, do not own it," *India Daily*, October 7, 2004.

Mintchik, Natalia M., "The Effect of SFAS NO. 141 AND SFAS NO. 142 on the Accuracy of Financial Analysts' Earnings Forecasts After Mergers," Dissertation, University of North Texas.

Moore, Karl, "Great Global Managers: They don't come from the Great Powers. Here's Where to Look," The Conference Board, 2005.

Mucha, Thomas, "A Motor City Marketing Lesson," *Business 2.0*, March 10, 2005.

"Navigating for Development," Managing in Times of Turbulence: An Executive Briefing, The Sixth Annual CEO Forum, Beijing, October 2002, Tuck School of Business at Dartmouth. William F. Achtmeyer Center for Global Leadership.

Nicolle, Lindsay, "Compliance: Make it Work for You," Computer-Weekly.com, July 13, 2004.

Ohmae, Kenichi, *The Borderless World*, HarperBusiness, 1999 with thanks to Starks, Rory, Aerdo Occasional Papers, "The Impact of Globalization on International Relief and Development," June 8, 2000 for bringing it to my attention.

On The Media, April 8, 2005 http://www.onthemedia.org/transcripts/transcripts_040805_chaos.html

Orr, Andrea, "Lost in Translation," CMO Magazine, May 2005.

"Financial Executives Call Sarbanes-Oxley Compliance a 'Good Investment,' According to Oversight Survey," Press Release of Oversight Systems, Inc. December 14, 2004.

Perdikou, Kim, "Reassessing the CIO," *CIO Asia*, May 2005.

Peters, Tom, "When All Plans Go Awry." http://www.tompeters.com/col_entries.php?note=005155&year=1986, July 1986.

Penhirin, Jacques, "Understanding the Chinese Consumer," Special Edition: What global executives think, The McKinsey Quarterly, 2004.

Pfeffer, Jeffrey, "The Real Keys to High Performance" *Leader to Leader*, No. 8, Spring 1998.

Prahalad, C.K., "Why Selling to the Poor Makes For Good Business," *Fortune*, Wednesday, November 3, 2004.

Rabinowitz, Robert, "Sympathy for the Devil? A Review of Jeffrey E. Garten's *The Mind of the CEO*." New York. Basic Books, 2001. Also *The Mind of the CEO*, pp 192–3.

Rao, S.L., "Life and Death of Brands," *The Telegraph*, Calcutta, India, June 6, 2005.

Rapier, Stephen M, "A Perspective on Turning 'David' into 'Goliath' for Sustained Growth," Stephen Rapier, The Artime Group, January 3, 2003.

Reichlin, Igor, "Getting the Global View," *Chief Executive*, October 2004.

Richardson, Bill, "How to Negotiate with Really Tough Guys," *Fortune*, May 27, 1996.

"Riding the Wave: The New Global Career Culture," Findings from Career Innovation Research. June 1999.

Rocks, David, "Dell's Second Web Revolution," *BusinessWeek*, September 18, 2000.

Rodrik, Dani, "Globalization, Growth and Poverty: Is the World Bank Beginning to Get It?" Dec 6, 2001.

Root, James and Smith, John. "Matching Global Growth to Industry Structure," Bain & Company, European Business Forum, Issue 14, July 2003.

Rosenbaum, Andrew, "How 'Ugly Americans' Can Play by Local Rules," *Harvard Business School Working Knowledge*, January 13, 2003.

Rothbard, Murray N., "Science, Technology and Government," The Mises Institute, March 1959. Previously unpublished. Copyright 2004.

Salacuse, Jeswald, "Negotiating: The top ten ways that culture can affect your negotiation," *Ivey Business Journal*, The University of Western Ontario, March/April 2005.

"Section 404 and Beyond: Documenting a More Effective and Efficient Approach to Compliance," BizNet Software, Inc, 2004.

Sebenius, James, "How to Negotiate "Yes" Across Cultural Boundaries," *Harvard Business School Working Knowledge*, April 8, 2002.

Sellers, Patricia, "Home Depot: Something to Prove," *Fortune*, June 27, 2002.

Shein, Esther, "The Knowledge Crunch," *CIO Magazine*, May 1, 2001.

Jeroen van der Veer, Shell Oil, "Introduction to Global Scenarios to 2025," www.shell.com.

Sirkin, Harold L. and George Stalk Jr, "Avoiding Supply Chain Shipwrecks: Navigating Outsourcing's Rocky Shoals," Boston Consulting Group, March 2005.

The Southern Institute, "Leading with Integrity," Presentation conducted by The Southern Institute in partnership with the Commerce Club, October 22, 2004. http://www.southerninstitute.org/Resources-GoodBusiness-Content(36).htm.

http://www.staffs.ac.uk/feo/documents/business_case.pdf.

Standard &Poor's, "Brazil Faces Challenges On The Road To Improved Creditworthiness," http://www.securitization.net/pdf/sp/Brazil_Faces_22Mar05.pdf, March 22, 2005.

Stodder, David, "Transitions and the Fortune 500," *The Intelligent Enterprise*, November, 1998, Volume 1, Number 2.

"Supply-chain management," *The Economist*, May 7, 2002.

Taylor, David A., "The New Competition," *Supply Chains—A Manager's Guide*, Addison-Wesley, 2004.

Tracy, William, "Made In Saudi Arabia," The Saudi Aramco World, May/June 1974.

Useeum, Michael, "Global Governance: The View from the 2005 World Economic Forum in Davos," DIEU (Danish International Continuing Education).

Useem, Jerry, "Exxon's African Adventure," *Fortune Magazine*, March 31, 2002.

Vodafone News Release, "Update on Adoption of International Financial Reporting Standards." January 20, 2005 http://www.vodafone.com/assets/files/en/IFRS_pr_final.pdf.

Watkins, Kevin, "Making Globalization Work for the Poor," *Finance & Development*, International Monetary Fund, March 2002.

"What, if Anything, Will Sink the Global Economy?," *Knowledge@Wharton*, Wharton School of Business, University of Pennsylvania, December 15, 2004.

Wrolstad, Jay, "Bloodbath at IBM," Newsfactor.com, May 5, 2005.

Wylie, Ian, "There is No Alternative . . . ," *Fast Company*, Issue 60, July 2002, page 106.

Endnotes

[1]Robert Rabinowitz. "Sympathy for the Devil? A Review of Jeffrey E. Garten's *The Mind of the CEO.*" New York. Basic Books, 2001. Also *The Mind of the CEO*, pp 192–3.

[2]Ibid.

[3]Dani Rodrik. "Globalization, Growth and Poverty: Is the World Bank Beginning to Get It?" Dec 6, 2001.

[4]Development and Globalization: Facts and Figures 2004, UNCTAD, and *Trade and Development Report 2002*, UNCTad.

[5]"Navigating for Development." Managing in Times of Turbulence: An Executive Briefing. The Sixth Annual CEO Forum, Beijing, October 2002. Tuck School of Business at Dartmouth. William F. Achtmeyer Center for Global Leadership.

[6]Standard & Poor's "Brazil Faces Challenges On The Road To Improved Creditworthiness," March 22, 2005.

[7]Nayan Chanda, "What Is Globalization" Yale Center for the Study of Globalization.

[8]"Why Selling to the Poor Makes For Good Business." C.K. Prahalad. *Fortune*, Wednesday, November 3, 2004.

[9]Jeff Hemerling, Dave Young. "Navigating the Five Currents of Globalization: How Leading Companies Are Capturing Global Advantage. Boston Consulting Group. January 2005.

[10]Peter Engardio and Dexter Roberts. "The China Price." *BusinessWeek*. Special Report. December 6, 2004.

[11]Jeff Hemerling, Dave Young. "Navigating the Five Currents of Globalization: How Leading Companies Are Capturing Global Advantage. Boston Consulting Group. January 2005.

[12]"The China Price".

[13]"Navigating the Five Currents of Globalization.".

[14]Interview with Mr. Katsuaki Watanabe, President, Toyota Motor Company, October 19, 2005.

[15]Interview with Mr. Kunio Nakamura, President, Matsushita Electric Industrial Co., Ltd, August 22, 2005.

[16]Stodder, David, "Transitions and the Fortune 500," *The Intelligent Enterprise*. November, 1998, Volume 1, Number 2.

[17]Interview with Mr Katsuaki Watanabe, President of Toyota Motor Company, October 19, 2005.

[18]Interview with Mr. Kunio Nakamura, President, Matsushita Electric Industrial Co., Ltd, August 22, 2005.

[19]Business Innovation Consortium, http://www.bicnow.com/what/EVPPOV.pdf.

[20]Capelli, Peter, "The Futility of Golden Handcuffs" *Harvard Business Review*.

[21]Charan, Ram, "Managing to Be Best." *Time Magazine*, http://www.time.com/time/time100/builder/other/managers.html.

[22]John Jewkes, David Sawers and Richard Stillerman, *The Sources of Invention* (1958; 2nd ed., 1969).

[23]Rothbard, Murray N., "Science, Technology and Government." The Mises Institute. March 1959. Previously unpublished. Copyright 2004.

[24]Peters, Tom. "When All Plans Go Awry." July 1986.

[25]Hammonds, Keith H. "Size is Not a Strategy," *Fast Company*. September 2002, Issue 62.

[26]Interview with Arvind Sodhani, President, Intel Capital, July 22, 2005.

[27]Boyer, Nicole, Global Business Network, "Reperceiving Business From the Bottom Up." GBN Working Paper. 2003.

[28]Charan, Ram, "Managing to Be Best." *Time Magazine,* http://www.time.com/time/time100/builder/other/managers.html.

[29]KPMG LLP (U.S.) "M&A Forum Highlights" March 2005.

[30]Pfeffer, Jeffrey, "The Real Keys to High Performance" *Leader to Leader,* No. 8 Spring 1998. (Ed: put a period after performance?).

[31]*HR Magazine,* April 1996.

[32]http://www.homedepot.com/HDUS/EN_US/corporate/about/eoc.shtml.

[33]Ibid.

[34]http://www.staffs.ac.uk/feo/documents/business_case.pdf.

[35]Dorf, Paul. R. Compensation Resources, Inc. Press Release. Sept, 2004.

[36]Lagace, Martha, "How to Put Meaning Back into Leading." HBS Working Knowledge, HBSWK Pub. Date: Jan 10, 2005. Interview with Joel M. Podolny, Rakesh Khurana, and Marya Hill-Popper.

[37]Riding the Wave: The New Global Career Culture. Findings from Career Innovation Research. June 1999.

[38]Goodall, Keith and Burgers, Willem, "Frequent Fliers" *China Business Review,* March 1998.

[39]Melvin, Sheila, Special Report: Human Resources, "Retaining Chinese Employees," *China Business Review,* November–December 2001.

[40]"Best Workplaces 2005," *Financial Times,* April 27, 2005.

[41]Interview with Katsuaki Watanabe, President of Toyota Motor Company, October 19, 2005.

[42]Ibid.

[43]Pfeffer, Jeffrey, "The Real Keys to High Performance" *Leader to Leader,* No. 8 Spring 1998. (Ed: same question as above).

[44]Boyes, William. *The New Managerial Economics,* Chapter Ten, The Firm's Architecture: Organization and Corporate Culture, Houghton Mifflin. 2003.

[45]Flynn, Tim and McCarthy, Mary Pat. *Risk: From the CEO and Board Perspective.* McGraw-Hill, 2003.

[46]Lagace, Martha, "How to Put Meaning Back into Leading." HBS Working Knowledge, HBSWK Pub. Date: Jan 10, 2005. Interview with Joel M. Podolny, Rakesh Khurana, and Marya Hill-Popper.

[47]"The Development Gateway Special Report: Foreign Investment and Development—Who Gains?" *Development Gateway*, February 21, 2005.

[48]Ibid.

[49]Ibid.

[50]"Building a Great Company," World Economic Forum, Davos, Switzerland, January 2005.

[51]Rocks, David, "Dell's Second Web Revolution," *BusinessWeek*, September 18, 2000.

[52]Breen, Bill, "Living in Dell Time," *Fast Company*, November, 2004, Issue 88.

[53]Ibid.

[54]Interview with Jim Owens and Dave Burritt, CEO and CFO of Caterpillar Inc., July 18, 2005.

[55]Interview with Katsuaki Watanabe, Toyota Motor Company, October 19, 2005.

[56]Knuchel, Francois, "CAMI Technology Transfer Project," Synergy Associates.

[57]"IBM Plans Restructuring Actions to Accelerate Global Integration of Operations, Company Will Take Second-Quarter Charge," IBM Press Release, May 4, 2005.

[58]Wrolstad, Jay, "Bloodbath at IBM," Newsfactor.com, May 5, 2005.

[59]Hamm, Steve, "IBM: More than Emergency Surgery," *BusinessWeek Online*, May 5, 2005.

[60]"The Compliance Journey: Balancing Risk and Controls with Business Improvement," KPMG LLP, 2004.

[61]Reilly, Kevin, "AMR Research Estimates Sarbanes-Oxley Spending Will Reach $5.8 billion in 2005," Press Release, AMR Research, November 12, 2004.

[62] AMR Research, Study, www.amrresearch.com.

[63] "Section 404 and Beyond: Documenting a More Effective and Efficient Approach to Compliance," BizNet Software, Inc, 2004.

[64] Shein, Esther, "The Knowledge Crunch," CIO Magazine, May 1, 2001.

[65] Ibid.

[66] Ibid.

[67] Flynn, Tim and McCarthy, Mary Pat, *Risk From the CEO and Board Perspective*, McGraw-Hill, 2003.

[68] Iritani, Evelyn and Dickerson, Marla, "Tallying Port Dispute's Costs," *Los Angeles Times*, November 25, 2002.

[69] Ibid.

[70] Interview with Mr. Kunio Nakamura, President, Matsushita Electric Industrial Co., Ltd, August 22, 2005.

[71] Interview with Stefan Krause, CFO, BMW Group, August 2, 2005.

[72] "Supply-chain management," *The Economist*, May 7, 2002.

[73] Dawson, Chester, "A China Price for Toyota," BusinessWeekOnline, February 21, 2005.

[74] Interview with Toyota Motor Company President, Katsuaki Watanabe, October 19, 2005.

[75] Lee, Hau L., "The Triple-A Supply Chain," *Harvard Business Review*, Vol. 82, No. 10, October 2004.

[76] Taylor, David A., "The New Competition," *Supply Chains—A Manager's Guide*, Addison-Wesley, 2004.

[77] Interview with Stefan Krause, CFO, BMW Group, August 2, 2005.

[78] Hagel, John III, "Offshoring goes on the offensive," *The McKinsey Quarterly*, 2004, Number 2.

[79] Mann, Catherine L., "Globalization of IT Services and White Collar Jobs: The Next Wave of Productivity Growth" *International Economics Policy Briefs*, Number PB03-11, December 2003.

[80] Aron, Ravi, Remarks before the 2005 World Economic Forum, Davos Switzerland.

[81]Ibid.

[82]Canon, Michael, Remarks before the 2005 World Economic Forum, Davos, Switzerland.

[83]EBS, "Offshore Outsourcing Basics," http://www.ebstrategy.com/outsourcing/basics/definition.htm.

[84]Mehta, Sankar, "GE's outsourcing departure sets a new trend—outsource headaches, do not own it," *India Daily*, October 7, 2004.

[85]Ibid.

[86]Craumer, Martha, "How to Think Strategically About Outsourcing," *Harvard Management Update*, Vol. 7, No. 5, May 2002.

[87]http://www.aaaa.org/transcripts/transcripts.html.

[88]On The Media, April 8, 2005 http://www.onthemedia.org/transcripts/transcripts_040805_chaos.html.

[89]Ohmae, Kenichi, The Borderless World, HarperBusiness, 1999 with thanks to Starks, Rory, Aerdo Occasional Papers, "The Impact of Globalization on International Relief and Development," June 8, 2000.

[90]Orr, Andrea, "Lost in Translation," *CMO Magazine*, May 2005.

[91]Ibid.

[92]Colyer, Edwin, "Prescribing a Global Identity," Brandchannel.com.

[93]Ibid.

[94]Dawson, Chester, *Lexus: The Relentless Pursuit*, John Wiley & Sons, 2004.

[95]Penhirin, Jacques, "Understanding the Chinese Consumer," *The McKinsey Quarterly*, 2004 Special Edition: What global executives think.

[96]Rao, S.L., "Life and Death of Brands," *The Telegraph*, Calcutta, India, June 6, 2005.

[97]Ibid.

[98]Business Today, August 7–21, 2000.

[99]Hyndai.co.in, Press release, "Hyundai achieves 105% domestic growth in April–May period," June 2005.

[100]Jain, Kuldeep; Manson, Nigel; Sankhe, Shirish, "The right passage to India," *The McKinsey Quarterly*, February 2005.

[101]Kirkpatrick, David; Roth, Daniel, "10 Tech Trends: Why There's No Escaping the Blog," *Fortune Magazine*, December 27, 2004.

[102]Ibid.

[103]Bialik, Carl, "Measuring the Impact of Blogs Requires More Than Just Counting," *The Wall Street Journal Online*, May 26, 2005.

[104]Mucha, Thomas, "A Motor City Marketing Lesson," Business 2.0, March 10, 2005.

[105]Ibid.

[106]Carlotti Jr., Stephen J; Coe, Mary Ellen, and Perrey, Jesko, "Making Brand Portfolios Work," The McKinsey Quarterly, 2004, Number 4.

[107]Hornblower, Sam, "Wal-Mart & China: A Joint Venture," supplement to the documentary "Is Wal-Mart Good for America?" by Frontline for WGBH Public Broadcasting, November 23, 2004.

[108]Interview with Arvind Sodhani, President, Intel Capital, July 22, 2005.

[109]Perdikou, Kim, "Reassessing the CIO," CIO Asia, May 2005.

[110]Ibid.

[111]Interview with Mr. Kunio Nakamura, President, Matsushita Electric Industrial Co., Ltd, August 22, 2005.

[112]Root, James; Smith, John. "Matching Global Growth to Industry Structure," Bain & Company, European Business Forum, Issue 14, July 2003.

[113]Ibid, p 84.

[114]Interview with Stefan Krause, CFO, BMW Group, August 2, 2005.

[115]"Global Footprint Design—Mastering the Rules of International Value Creation," Study, June 2004.

[116]Kothar, S.P.; Libert, Barry, "Value of Investment in Intangibles," MIT Sloan Management Review, Fall 2001, Vol. 43, No. 1.

[117]Mintchik, Natalia M., "The Effect of SFAS NO. 141 AND SFAS NO. 142 on the Accuracy of Financial Analysts' Earnings Forecasts After Mergers," Dissertation, University of North Texas.

[118]Vodafone News Release, "Update on Adoption of International Financial Reporting Standards." January 20, 2005 http://www.vodafone.com/assets/files/en/IFRS_pr_final.pdf.

[119]http://bwnt.businessweek.com/brand/2005/.

[120]http://www.ibm.com/news/us/en/2005/01/patents.html.

[121]KPMG International, "The Compliance Journey: Making Compliance Sustainable," 2005 and KPMG International, "The Compliance Journey: Balancing Risk and Controls with Business Improvement," 2004.

[122]Nicolle, Lindsay, "Compliance: Make it Work for You," Computer-Weekly.com, July 13, 2004.

[123]Financial Executives Call Sarbanes-Oxley Compliance a 'Good Investment,' According to Oversight Survey," Press Release of Oversight Systems, Inc. December 14, 2004.

[124]Bialik, Carl, "How Much is it Really Costing to Comply with Sarbanes-Oxley?" Wall Street Journal Online, June 16, 2005.

[125]KPMG International, "The Compliance Journey: Making Compliance Sustainable," 2005 and KPMG International, "The Compliance Journey: Balancing Risk and Controls with Business Improvement," 2004.

[126]Useeum, Michael, "Global Governance: The View from the 2005 World Economic Forum in Davos," DIEU (Danish International Continuing Education).

[127]Ibid.

[128]"What, if Anything, Will Sink the Global Economy?," Knowledge@Wharton, Wharton School of Business, University of Pennsylvania, December 15, 2004.

[129]Ibid.

[130]Interview with Mr. Kunio Nakamura, President, Matsushita Electric Industrial Co., Ltd, August 22, 2005.

[131]KPMG International, "The Compliance Journey: Making Compliance Sustainable," 2005, page 4.

[132]Daum, Juergen, H., "How Scenario Planning Can Significantly Reduce Strategic Risks and Boost Value in the Innovation Chain." The New Economist Analyst Report September 8, 2001.

[133]Ibid.

[134]Wylie, Ian, "There is No Alternative . . . ," Fast Company, Issue 60, July 2002, page 106.

[135]Fuld, Leonard, "Business Tsunamis are Approaching. Learn How to Prepare." Pharmaceutical Executive, May 1, 2004.

[136]Kleiner, Art, "The Man Who Saw the Future," Strategy + Business, Spring 2003.

[137]Groundwater, Fergus, "The Branham Leadership Series: Management Strategies for Success in IT's Turbulent Times," and Zook, Chris and Rigby, Darrell, "How to Think Strategically in a Recession," Harvard Management Update, November 2001.

[138]Fuld, Leonard, "Business Tsunamis are Approaching. Learn How to Prepare." Pharmaceutical Executive, May 1, 2004.

[139]Hoblitzell, Tom, "CEO Perspectives: Business Planning in Inclement Economic Weather," DM Review Magazine, June, 2002.

[140]Hafrey, Leigh, "Proseminar on Narrative, Ethics, and Teaching in the Workplace." Also Shaw, Gordon and Brown, Robert, "Strategic Stories: How 3M is Rewriting Business Planning," Harvard Business Review, May–June 1998.

[141]Useem, Jerry, "Exxon's African Adventure," Fortune, March 31, 2002.

[142]Ibid.

[143]Ibid.

[144]Sebenius, James, "How to Negotiate "Yes" Across Cultural Boundaries," Harvard Business School Working Knowledge, April 8, 2002.

[145]Ibid.

[146]Rosenbaum, Andrew, "How 'Ugly Americans' Can Play by Local Rules," Harvard Business School Working Knowledge, January 13, 2003.

[147]Liss, David, "Bill Richardson: 'Find the Common Thread,'" BusinessWeek online, November 13, 2003.

[148]Kinsey Goman, Carol, "Five reasons people don't tell what they know," Knowledge Management, June 2, 2002 http://www.kmmag.com/articles/default.asp?ArticleID=960.

[149]Ibid.

[150]"You have to be Pushy and Aggressive," BusinessWeek, February 24, 1997.

[151]Salacuse, Jeswald, "Negotiating: The top ten ways that culture can affect your negotiation," Ivey Business Journal, The University of Western Ontario, March/April 2005.

[152]Maidment, Paul, "Washington Politics Shock Chinese," Forbes, August 2, 2005.

[153]Hanna, Julia, "MNCs in Asia: Investing in the Future," HBS Bulletin, February 25, 2002.

[154]Ibid.

[155]De Capele, Gaetan, "Une ligne de defense très politique," Le Figaro, July 20, 2005.

[156]Katz, David, "The Bribery Gap," CFO.com, January 1, 2005.

[157]"Corruption: Cutting the Cost of Doing Business," Africa Economic Summit, World Economic Forum, January 6, 2005.

[158]Interview with Jim Owens and Dave Burritt, CEO and CFO of Caterpillar Inc., July 18, 2005.

[159]Ibid.

[160]Ibid.

[161]Interview with Mr. Kunio Nakamura, President, Matsushita Electric Industrial Co., Ltd, August 22, 2005.

[162]Bradford, Roslyn, "Management Across Borders," Alumni Profiles, University of Southern California.

[163]Moore, Karl, "Great Global Managers: They don't come from the Great Powers. Here's Where to Look," The Conference Board, 2005.

[164]Ibid.

[165]Buss, Dale, "Non-American CEOs are having a big impact at traditional U.S. companies," Chief Executive, April 2004.

[166]Building High-Potential Leaders Study, Hewitt, http://was4.hewitt.com/hewitt/resource/articleindex/talent/grooming.htm.

[167]Reichlin, Igor, "Getting the Global View," Chief Executive Magazine, October 2004.

[168]Ibid.

[169]Sellers, Patricia, "Home Depot: Something to Prove," Fortune, June 27, 2002.

[170]Ibid.

[171]Interview with Stefan Krause, CFO of BMW Group, August 2005.

[172]Conger, Jay and Fulmer, Robert, "Bench Strength: Grooming Your Next CEO," Harvard Business School, Working Knowledge, January 19, 2004. Based on an excerpt from "Developing Your Leadership Pipeline," Harvard Business Review, December 2003.

[173]George, Bill, "Becoming a leader of heart and soul," Address to Stanford University's Graduate School of Business, April 2004.

Index

About the Authors

Hiroaki Yoshihara is a Vice Chair and Global Managing Partner at KPMG International, responsible for global industry and client initiatives. Hiro is a member of the International Executive Team. He has over 25 years of experience serving many global clients and has significant experience in the area of business strategy and mergers and acquisitions. He is coauthor of *Successful Performance Management*. Now based in London, he remains active in global business organizations such as the World Economic Forum and the U.S.-Japan Business Council, and has often appeared in leading media such as TV Tokyo and Nikkei publications. Hiro also served as visiting professor at the Kobe University Graduate School of Business.

Mary Pat McCarthy is Vice Chair of Industries at KPMG LLP (U.S.). She is a member of the U.S. firm's management committee and a business advisor to many of the world's largest high technology and telecommunications companies. She is coauthor of four leading business books that have covered an array of critical business issues—*Risk from the CEO and Board Perspective, Agile Business for Fragile Times, Security Transformation,* and *Digital Transformation*. Mary Pat is active in various organizations and has served on the Digital Divide Task Force at the World Economic Forum.